TELEPATHY
and
THE ETHERIC VEHICLE

BOOKS BY ALICE A. BAILEY

Initiation, Human and Solar
Letters on Occult Meditation
The Consciousness of the Atom
A Treatise on Cosmic Fire
The Light of the Soul
The Soul and Its Mechanism
From Intellect to Intuition
A Treatise on White Magic
From Bethlehem to Calvary
Discipleship in the New Age — Vol. I
Discipleship in the New Age — Vol. II
Problems of Humanity
The Reappearance of the Christ
The Destiny of the Nations
Glamour: A World Problem
Telepathy and the Etheric Vehicle
The Unfinished Autobiography
Education in the New Age
The Externalisation of the Hierarchy
A Treatise on the Seven Rays:
  Vol. I — Esoteric Psychology
  Vol. II — Esoteric Psychology
  Vol. III — Esoteric Astrology
  Vol. IV — Esoteric Healing
  Vol. V — Rays and Initiations

TELEPATHY

AND

THE ETHERIC VEHICLE

by
ALICE A. BAILEY

LUCIS PUBLISHING COMPANY
New York

LUCIS PRESS, Ltd.
London

First Printing, 1950
Sixth Printing, 1971 (First Paperback Edition)
Thirteenth Printing, 2008

ISBN No. 0-85330-116-6
Library of Congress Catalog Card Number: 50-11465

The publication of this book is financed by the Tibetan Book Fund which is established for the perpetuation of the teachings of the Tibetan and Alice A. Bailey.

This Fund is controlled by the Lucis Trust, a tax-exempt, religious, educational corporation.

The Lucis Publishing Company is a non-profit organisation owned by the Lucis Trust. No royalties are paid on this book.

This title is also available
in a clothbound edition.

It has been translated into Danish, Dutch, French, German, Greek, Hungarian, Italian, Japanese, Portuguese, Russian, Serbo-Croatian, Spanish, and Swedish. Translation into other languages is proceeding.

LUCIS PUBLISHING COMPANY
120 Wall Street
New York, NY 10005

LUCIS PRESS, Ltd.
Suite 54
3 Whitehall Court
London SW1A 2EF

MANUFACTURED IN THE UNITED STATES OF AMERICA

EXTRACT FROM A STATEMENT BY THE TIBETAN

Published August 1934

Suffice it to say, that I am a Tibetan disciple of a certain degree, and this tells you but little, for all are disciples from the humblest aspirant up to, and beyond, the Christ Himself. I live in a physical body like other men, on the borders of Tibet, and at times (from the exoteric standpoint) preside over a large group of Tibetan lamas, when my other duties permit. It is this fact that has caused it to be reported that I am an abbot of this particular lamasery. Those associated with me in the work of the Hierarchy (and all true disciples are associated in this work) know me by still another name and office. A.A.B. knows who I am and recognises me by two of my names.

I am a brother of yours, who has travelled a little longer upon the Path than has the average student, and has therefore incurred greater responsibilities. I am one who has wrestled and fought his way into a greater measure of light than has the aspirant who will read this article, and I must therefore act as a transmitter of the light, no matter what the cost. I am not an old man, as age counts among the teachers, yet I am not young or inexperienced. My work is to teach and spread the knowledge of the Ageless Wisdom wherever I can find a response, and I have been doing this for many years. I seek also to help the Master M. and the Master K.H. whenever opportunity offers, for I have been long connected with Them and with Their work. In all the above, I have told you much; yet at the same time I have told you nothing which would lead you to offer me that blind obedience and the foolish devotion which the emotional aspirant offers to the Guru and Master whom he is as yet unable to contact. Nor will he make that desired contact until he has transmuted emotional devotion into unselfish service to humanity,—not to the Master.

The books that I have written are sent out with no claim for their acceptance. They may, or may not, be correct, true and useful. It is for you to ascertain their truth by right practice and by the exercise of the intuition. Neither I nor A.A.B. is the least interested in having them acclaimed as inspired writings, or in having anyone speak of them (with bated breath) as being the work of one of the Masters. If they present truth in such a way that it follows sequentially upon that already offered in the world teachings, if the information given raises the aspiration and the will-to-serve from the plane of the emotions to that of the mind (the plane whereon the Masters *can* be found) then they will have served their purpose. If the teaching conveyed calls forth a response from the illumined mind of the worker in the world, and brings a flashing forth of his intuition, then let that teaching be accepted. But not otherwise. If the statements meet with eventual corroboration, or are deemed true under the test of the Law of Correspondences, then that is well and good. But should this not be so, let not the student accept what is said.

CONTENTS

SECTION ONE

TEACHING ON TELEPATHY

SECTION TWO

TEACHING ON THE ETHERIC VEHICLE

THE GREAT INVOCATION

From the point of Light within the Mind of God
    Let light stream forth into the minds of men.
    Let Light descend on Earth.

From the point of Love within the Heart of God
    Let love stream forth into the hearts of men.
    May Christ return to Earth.

From the centre where the Will of God is known
    Let purpose guide the little wills of men —
    The purpose which the Masters know and serve.

From the centre which we call the race of men
    Let the Plan of Love and Light work out
    And may it seal the door where evil dwells.

Let Light and Love and Power restore the Plan on Earth.

"The above Invocation or Prayer does not belong to any person or group but to all Humanity. The beauty and the strength of this Invocation lies in its simplicity, and in its expression of certain central truths which all men, innately and normally, accept—the truth of the existence of a basic Intelligence to Whom we vaguely give the name of God; the truth that behind all outer seeming, the motivating power of the universe is Love; the truth that a great Individuality came to earth, called by Christians, the Christ, and embodied that love so that we could understand; the truth that both love and intelligence are effects of what is called the Will of God; and finally the self-evident truth that only through *humanity* itself can the Divine Plan work out."

ALICE A. BAILEY

THE SEVEN PLANES OF OUR SOLAR SYSTEM

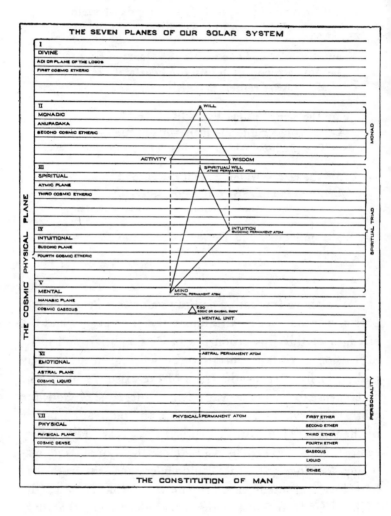

THE CONSTITUTION OF MAN

EVOLUTION OF A SOLAR LOGOS

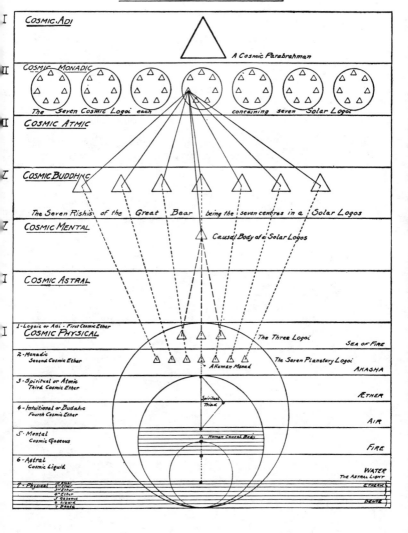

TEACHING ON TELEPATHY

I. THE FIELD OF TELEPATHIC INTERPLAY

One of the characteristics, distinguishing the group of world servers and knowers, is that the outer organisation which holds them integrated is practically non-existent. They are *held together by an inner structure of thought* and by a telepathic medium of inter-relation. The Great Ones, Whom we all seek to serve, are thus linked, and can—at the slightest need and with the least expenditure of force—get en rapport with each other. They are all tuned to a particular vibration.

In the new groups are collected together people who are very diverse in their nature, who are found upon differing rays, who are of different nationalities, and who are each of them the product of widely varying environments and heredity. Besides these obvious factors which immediately attract attention, there is also to be found an equal diversity in the life experience of the souls concerned. The complexity of the problem is also tremendously increased when one remembers the long road which each has travelled and the many factors (emerging out of a dim and distant past) which have contributed to make each person what he now is. When, therefore, one dwells on the barriers and difficulties supervening upon such diverse conditions, the question arises at once: What provides the common meeting ground, and what makes it possible to have an interplay between the minds involved? The answer to this question is of paramount importance and necessitates a clear understanding.

When the Biblical words are used: "In Him we live and move and have our being," we have the statement of a fundamental law in nature and the enunciated basis of the fact which we cover by the rather meaningless word: *Omnipresence*. Omnipresence has its basis in the substance of the universe, and in what the scientists call the ether; this word "ether" is a generic term covering the ocean of energies which are all inter-related and which constitute that one synthetic energy body of our planet.

In approaching, therefore, the subject of telepathy, it must be carefully borne in mind that the etheric body of every form in nature is an integral part of the substantial form of God Himself—not the dense physical form, but what the esotericists regard as the form-making substance. We use the word God to signify the expression of the One Life which animates every form on the outer objective plane. The etheric or energy body, therefore, of every human being is an integral part of the etheric body of the planet itself and consequently of the solar system. Through this medium, every human being is basically related to every other expression of the Divine Life, minute or great. The function of the etheric body is to receive energy impulses and to be swept into activity by these impulses, or streams of force, emanating from some originating source or other. The etheric body is in reality naught but energy. It is composed of myriads of threads of force or tiny streams of energy, held in relation to the emotional and mental bodies and to the soul by their co-ordinating effect. These streams of energy, in their turn, have an effect on the physical body and swing it into activity of some kind or another, according to the nature and power of whatever type of energy may be dominating the etheric body at any particular time.

Through the etheric body, therefore, circulates energy emanating from some mind. With humanity in the mass, response is made unconsciously to the rulings of the Universal Mind; this is complicated in our time and age by a growing responsiveness to the mass ideas—called sometimes public opinion—of the rapidly evolving human mentality. Within the human family are also found those who respond to that inner group of Thinkers Who, working in mental matter, control from the subjective side of life the emergence of the great plan and the manifestation of divine purpose.

This group of Thinkers falls into seven main divisions and is presided over by three great Lives or super-conscious Entities. These three are the Manu, the Christ, and the Mahachohan. These three work primarily through the method of influencing the minds of the adepts and the initiates. These latter in their turn influence the disciples of the world, and these disciples, each in his own place and on his own responsibility, work out their concept of the plan and seek to give expression to it as far as possible. It is, therefore, as you can surmise, a process of stepping down rates of vibration until they are sufficiently heavy to affect physical plane matter and thus make possible the building of organised effects on the physical plane. These disciples have hitherto worked very much alone except when karmic relationships have revealed them to each other, and telepathic intercommunication has been fundamentally confined to the Hierarchy of adepts and initiates, both in and out of incarnation, and to Their individual work with Their disciples.

It is, however, now deemed possible to establish a resembling condition and a telepathic relation between disciples on the physical plane. No matter where they may find themselves, this group of mystics and knowers will eventually find it feasible to communicate with one another and frequently do even now. A basic mystical idea or some new revelation of truth is suddenly recognised by many and finds expression simultaneously through the medium of many minds. No one person can claim individual right to the enunciated principle or truth. Several minds have registered it. It is usually stated, however, in a wide generalisation, that these people have tapped the inner thought currents or have responded to the play of the Universal Mind. Literally and technically this is not so. The Universal Mind is tapped by some member of the planetary Hierarchy according to His mental bias and equipment, and the immediate needs sensed by the working adepts. He then presents the new idea, new discovery, or the new revelation to the group of adepts (telepathically, of course, my brother) and, when it has been discussed by them, He later presents it to His group of disciples. Among them He will find one who responds more readily and intelligently than the others and this one, through his clear thinking and the power of his formulated thoughtforms, can then influence other minds. These others grasp the concept as theirs; they seize upon it and work it out into manifestation. Each regards it as his special privilege so to do and, because of this specialising faculty and his automatically engendered responsibility, he throws back of it all the energy which is his, and works and fights for his thoughtforms.

An illustration of this is to be found in the history of the League of Nations. Before He took up special work, the Master Serapis sought to bring through some constructive idea for the helping of humanity. He conceived of a world unity in the realm of politics which would work out as an intelligent banding of the nations for the preservation of international peace. He presented it to the adepts in conclave and it was felt that something could be done.

The Master Jesus undertook to present it to His group of disciples as He was working in the occident. One of these disciples on the inner planes, seized upon the suggestion and passed it on (or rather stepped it down) until it registered in the brain of Colonel House. He, not recording the source (of which he was totally unaware), passed it on in turn to that sixth ray aspirant, called Woodrow Wilson. Then, fed by the wealth of analogous ideas in the minds of many, it was presented to the world. It should be borne in mind that the function of a disciple is to focus a stream of energy of some special kind upon the physical plane where it can become an attractive centre of force and draw to itself similar types of ideas and thought currents which are not strong enough to live by themselves or to make a sufficiently strong impact upon the human consciousness.

In union is strength. This is the second law governing telepathic communication.

The first law is:

1. The power to communicate is to be found in the very nature of substance itself. It lies potentially within the ether, and the significance of telepathy is to be found in the word *omnipresence.*

The second law is:

2. The interplay of many minds produces a unity of thought which is powerful enough to be recognised by the brain.

Here we have a law governing a subjective activity and another law governing objective manifestation. Let us voice these laws in the simplest manner possible. When each member of the group can function in his mind-con-sciousness, untrammelled by the brain or the emotional nature, he will discover the universality of *the mental principle which is the first exoteric expression of the soul consciousness*. He will then enter into the world of ideas, becoming aware of them through the sensitive receiving plate of the mind. He then seeks to find those who respond to the same type of ideas and who react to the same mental impulse, simultaneously with himself. Uniting himself to them he discovers himself to be en rapport with them.

The understanding of the first law produces results in the mind or mental body. The understanding of the second law produces results in a lesser receiving station, the brain. This is possible through the strengthening of a man's own mental re-action by the mental re-action of others, similarly receptive. It will be found therefore that this process of communication, governed by these two laws, has always been in operation among the adepts, the initiates and the senior disciples who are in physical plane bodies. Now the operation of this process is to be extended and steadily developed by the emerging group of mystics and world servers who constitute, in embryo, the world Saviour.

Only those who know something of the meaning of concentration and meditation and who can hold the mind steady in the light will be able to understand the first law and comprehend that interplay of thought-directed energies which finds one terminal of expression in the mind of some inspired Thinker, and the other terminal in the mind of the attentive world server who seeks to tune in on those mind processes which hold the clue to ultimate world salvation. The thought-directing energy has for its source a Thinker Who can enter into the divine Mind, owing to His having transcended human limitation; the thought-directed receiver is the man, in exoteric expression, who has aligned his brain, his mind, and his soul.

It is a fact that omnipresence, which is a law in nature and based on the fact that the etheric bodies of all forms constitute the world etheric body, makes *omniscience* possible. The etheric body of the planetary Logos is swept into activity by His directed will; energy is the result of His thoughtform playing in and through His energy body. This thoughtform embodies and expresses His world Purpose. All the subhuman forms of life and the human forms up to the stage of advanced man are governed by divine thought through the medium of their energy bodies which are an integral part of the whole. They react, however, unconsciously and unintelligently. Advanced humanity, the mystics and the knowers, are becoming increasingly aware of the mind which directs the evolutionary process. When this awareness is cultivated and the individual mind is brought consciously into contact with the mind of God as it expresses itself through the illumined mind of the Hierarchy of adepts, we shall have the steady growth of omniscience. This is the whole story of telepathic interplay in the true sense; it portrays the growth of that oligarchy of elect souls who will eventually rule the world, who will be chosen so to rule, and who will be recognised by the mass as eligible for that high office through the co-ordination that they have established between:

1. The universal mind.
2. Their individual mind illumined by the soul consciousness.
3. The brain, reacting to the individual mind, and
4. The group of those whose minds and brains are similarly tuned and telepathically related.

In connection with disciples and aspirants to disciple-ship, it is presumed that their minds are somewhat attuned to the soul; that they are also so aligned that the soul, mind and brain are co-ordinated and are beginning to function as a unit. This is the individual responsibility. Now comes the task of learning to be responsive to the group and to find and contact those minds which are energised by similar thought currents. This has to be cultivated. How, my brother, shall this be done? Let us consider the various types of telepathic work.

The undeveloped human being and the unthinking, non-mental man or woman can be and often are telepathic, but the centre through which they work is the solar plexus. The line of communication is, therefore, from solar plexus to solar plexus. This is therefore *instinctual telepathy* and concerns *feeling* in every case. It involves, invariably, radi-ations from the solar plexus, which in the case of the animal world serves usually as the instinctual brain. This type of telepathic communication is definitely a characteristic of the animal body of man, and one of the best illustrations of this telepathic rapport is that existing between a mother and her child. It is this type of telepathy which is pre-dominantly present in the average spiritualistic seance. There the medium, quite unconsciously, sets up a telepathic rapport with the people in the circle. Their feelings, worries, sorrows, and desires become apparent and form part of the reading, so called. Both the sitters and the medium are functioning through the same centre. With this class of medium, and in this type of seance, the highly intelligent and mentally polarised man or woman will learn nothing, and will probably receive no messages, unless faked. Hence, therefore, when it comes to scientific investi-gation by trained minds, physical phenomena has predomi-nated and not the more subtle forms of psychism. Where the more subtle forms of super- or extra-sensory perception have been involved, the subjects have been either adolescent or in their early twenties and have been primarily and rightly focussed in the emotional-feeling body. This is true even when they are highly intellectual.

This form of telepathic communication is therefore of two kinds, with the solar plexus always involved:

a. It will be from solar plexus to solar plexus between two people who are ordinary, emotional, governed by desire, and primarily centred in the astral and animal bodies.

b. It will be between such a "solar plexus" person, if I may so call him, and a higher type whose solar plexus centre is functioning actively but whose throat centre is also alive. This type of person registers in two places—provided that the thought sensed and sent out by the solar plexus person has in it something of mental substance or energy. Pure feeling and entirely emotional emanations between people necessitate only solar plexus contact.

Later, when group work in telepathy is undertaken, the centres of transmission wherein high and consecrated feeling, devotion, aspiration and love are concerned and where the groups work with pure love, communication will be from heart to heart, and from a group heart to another group heart. The phrase "heart to heart talk," so often used, is usually a misnomer at this time, but will some day be true. At present it is usually a solar plexus conversation!

The second form of telepathic work is that of mind to mind, and it is with this form of communication that the highest investigation is at this time concerned. Only mental types are involved, and the more that emotion and feeling and strong desire can be eliminated, the more accurate will be the work accomplished. The strong desire to achieve success in telepathic work, and the fear of failure, are the surest ways to offset fruitful effort. In all such work as this, an attitude of non-attachment and a spirit of 'don't care' are of real assistance. Experimenters along this line need to give more time and thought to the recognition of types of force. They need to realise that emotion, and desire for anything, on the part of the receiving agent create streams of emanating energy which rebuff or repulse that which seeks to make contact, such as the directed thought of someone seeking rapport. When these streams are adequately strong, they act like a boomerang and return to the emanating centre, being attracted back there by the power of the vibration which sent them forth. In this thought lies hid the cause of :

a. The failure on the part of the broadcasting or trans-mitting agent. Intense desire to make a satisfactory impression will attract the outgoing thought back again to the transmitter.
b. The failure on the part of the receiving agent whose own intense desire to be successful sends out such a stream of outgoing energy that the stream of incom-ing energy is met, blocked and driven back whence it came; or, if the receiver is aware of this and seeks to stem the tide of his desire, he frequently succeeds in surrounding himself with a wall of inhibited desire through which naught can penetrate.

Telepathy and the allied powers will only be understood when the nature of force, of emanations and radiations, and of energy currents, is better grasped. This is rapidly coming about as science penetrates more deeply into the arcana of energies and begins to work—as does the occultist—in the world of forces.

It should also be borne in mind that it is only as the centres employed are consciously used that we have that carefully directed work which will be fruitful of results. For instance, an emotional person, using primarily the solar plexus centre, will be endeavouring to enter into rapport with a mental type. From this will result only confusion. The two parties concerned are using different centres and are sensitive to certain types of force and closed to others. Again, some people, even if mentally polarised and therefore sensitive to similar vibrations attempt to make a telepathic contact when one party is under emotional strain and therefore not responsive, or one party is intensively occupied with some mental problem and is encased in a wall of thoughtforms and therefore impervious to impressions. You can see, therefore, how a cultivation of detachment is a necessary qualification for success in telepathic work.

All who seek to tread the Path of Discipleship are endeavouring to live in the head centre, and—through meditation—to bring in the power of the soul. The problem which you face, as disciples learning telepathic sensitivity, is founded on two things:

a. Upon which of your three bodies is the most active; thereby is indicated where you live subjectively most of the time.

b. Upon which centre is the most expressive in your equipment, and through which you contact most easily modern living conditions. I mean by these words: where, literally speaking, your life energy is predominantly focussed and your sentient energy expresses itself the most.

An understanding of this will make you better able to work and to make intelligent experiment. Therefore, watch yourselves with care yet impersonally, and work out the why and the wherefore of the effects produced, for by this means you will learn.

The third type of telepathic work is that from soul to soul. This is the highest type of telepathic work possible to humanity and is that form of communication which has been responsible for all the inspirational writings of real power, the world Scriptures, the illumined utterances, the inspired speakers, and the language of symbolism. It only becomes possible where there is an integrated personality, and, at the same time, the power to focus oneself in the soul consciousness. The mind and the brain have, at the same time, to be brought into perfect rapport and alignment.

It is my intention to elucidate further this science of communication, which started through the sense of touch and developed through sound, symbols, words and sentences, languages, writing, art, and on again to the stage of higher symbols, vibratory contact, telepathy, inspiration and illumination. I have, however, in the above, dealt with the general outline and we will take the specific details later.

The work of the telepathic communicators is one of the most important in the coming new age, and it will be of value to gain some idea of its significance and techniques. I would, in summarising the above instruction, state that in connection with individuals:

1. Telepathic communication is
   a. Between soul and mind.
   b. Between soul, mind and brain.

This is as far as interior individual development is concerned.

2. When it is found between individuals, telepathic communication is
   a. Between soul and soul.
   b. Between mind and mind.
   c. Between solar plexus and solar plexus, and therefore purely emotional.
   d. Between all these three aspects of energy simultaneously, in the case of very advanced people.

3. Telepathic communication is also:
   a. Between a Master and His disciples or disciple.
   b. Between a Master and His group and a group or groups of sensitives and aspirants on the physical plane.
   e. Between subjective and objective groups.
   d. Between the occult Hierarchy and groups of disciples on the physical plane.
   e. Between the Hierarchy and the New Group of World Servers in order to reach humanity and lift it nearer the goal.

This concerns the new science of group telepathic communication, of which herd or mass telepathy (so well known) is the lowest known expression. This instinctual telepathy which is shown by a flight of birds, acting as a unit, or that animal telepathy which serves to govern so mysteriously the movements of herds of animals, and the rapid transmission of information among the savage races and non-intelligent peoples—these are all instances of that lower externalisation of an inner spiritual reality. An intermediate stage of this instinctual activity, based largely on solar plexus reactions, can be seen in modern mass psychology and public opinion. It is, as you know, predominantly emotional, unintelligent, astral and fluidic in its expression. This is changing rapidly and shifting into the realm of what is called "intelligent public opinion," but this is, as yet, slow. It involves the activity of the throat and ajna centres. We have, therefore:

1. Instinctual telepathy.
2. Mental telepathy.
3. Intuitional telepathy.

I would remind you right at the outset that sensitivity to the thoughts of one's Master, sensitivity to the world of ideas, and sensitivity to intuitional impressions are all forms of telepathic sensitivity.

In any consideration of this theme, it is obvious that there are three major factors which must be considered:

1. The *initiating agent*. I use this word with deliberate intent, as the power to work telepathically, both as initiating agent and as recipient, is closely connected with initiation, and is one of the indications that a man is ready for that process.

2. The *recipient* of that which is conveyed to him on the "wings of thought."

3. The *medium* through which it is intended to convey the transfer of thought, of idea, of wish, of imprint, and therefore of some form of knowledge.

This is the simplest statement of the elementary mechanics of the process. This indicates, likewise, the most elementary comprehension of the thought covered so frequently by the *Bhagavad Gita* in the words which we have translated in the West by the terms: the Knower, the Field of Knowledge, and the Known. You have oft been told that every sacred book, such as the *Bhagavad Gita,* for instance, has various interpretations, dependent upon the point in evolution of the reader, or seeker after truth. This interpretation of the *Bhagavad Gita* in terms of Communicator, Communication and Communicant still demands elucidation, and in the idea which I have above conveyed to you, I have given you a hint.

Let us now discuss in some detail the three types of telepathy enumerated above: instinctual telepathy, mental telepathy, and intuitional telepathy. These three produce differing modes of activity and tap (to use a familiar word) differing areas of communication.

1. *Instinctual telepathy* is based upon those impacts of energy which come from one etheric body and make an impression upon another. The medium of communication employed is, as we have seen, the etheric substance of all bodies, which is necessarily one with the etheric substance of the planet. The area around the solar plexus (though not in direct relation to that centre as it exists as an instrument differentiated from all other instruments or centres) is sensitive to the impact of etheric energy, for this area in the etheric body is in direct "touch" with the astral body, the feeling body. Also, close to the solar plexus is found that centre near the spleen which is the direct instrument for the entrance of *prana* into the human mechanism. This instinctual response to etheric contact was the mode of communication in Lemurian times, and largely took the place of thought and of speech. It concerned itself primarily with two types of impression: that which had to do with the instinct of self-preservation, and that which had to do with self-reproduction. A higher form of this instinctual telepathy has been preserved for us in the expression we so frequently use, "I have a feeling that . . . ," and allied phrases. These are more definitely astral in their implications and work through the astral substance, using the solar plexus area as a sensitive plate for impact and impression.

One point should here be made clear, and upon it you should ponder. This *astral* (not etheric) sensitivity, or "feeling telepathy" is basically the Atlantean mode of communication, and involved finally the use of the solar plexus centre itself as the receiving agent; the emitting agent (if I may use such a phrase) worked, however, through the entire area of the diaphragm. It was as though there appeared, through emergence, a gathering of forces or outgoing waves of energy in that part of the human vehicle. The relatively wide area from which the information was sent out acted as a large general distributor; the area which received the impression, however, was more localised, involving only the solar plexus. The reason for this can be found in the fact that in Atlantean days the human being was still unable to *think,* as we understand thinking. The whole lower part of the body, in a sense difficult for us to grasp, was given up to feeling; the communicator's one thought-contribution was the name of the recipient, plus the name or noun form of that which was the idea to be conveyed. This embryo thought winged its way to its goal, and the powerful "feeling" apparatus of the solar plexus received it (acting like a magnet) and drew the "feeling impression" powerfully there, drawing thus upon the communicator. It is this process which is pursued when, for instance, some mother "feels" that some danger threatens her child, or that some happening is taking place in connection with her child. She is thus sometimes enabled to send, by the medium of instinctual love, a most definite warning. The solar plexus is involved where the recipient is concerned; the area around the diaphragm is involved where the communicator is concerned.

2. In our race, the Aryan, instinctual telepathic work is still the major expression of this spiritual possibility, but at the same time *mental telepathy* is becoming increas-

ingly prevalent. This will be more and more so, as time goes on. It is most difficult in this transition period to define, or differentiate, the peculiar areas involved, because the solar plexus is still exceedingly active. What we have today is a mixture of instinctual telepathy and the beginning of mental telepathy. This manifests, however, very seldom, and then only in the educated classes. With the masses, instinctual telepathy is still the mode of contact. The throat centre is primarily involved where mental telepathy is concerned; there is also sometimes a little heart activity and always a measure of solar plexus reaction. Hence our problem. Frequently the communicator will send a message via the throat centre, and the recipient will still use the solar plexus. This is the most frequent method, and I would ask you to remember this. The sending out of a message may involve, and frequently does in connection with disciples, the throat centre, but the recipient will probably use the solar plexus centre. The throat centre is *the* centre, par excellence, or the medium, of all creative work. The heart and the throat, however, must eventually be used in synthesis. I stated the reason for this earlier in the words: "Only from the heart centre can stream, in reality, those lines of energy which link and bind together. It was for this reason that I have assigned certain meditations which stimulated the heart centre into action, linking the heart centre (between the shoulder blades) to the head centre, through the medium of the higher correspondence to the heart centre, found within the head centre (the thousand petalled lotus). This heart centre, when adequately radiatory and magnetic, relates disciples to each other and to all the world. It will also produce that telepathic interplay which is so much to be desired and which is so constructively useful to the spiritual Hierarchy— provided it is established within a group of pledged disciples, dedicated to the service of humanity. They can then be trusted."*

3. *Intuitional telepathy* is one of the developments upon the Path of Discipleship. It is one of the fruits of true meditation. The area involved is the head and throat, and the three centres which will be rendered active in the process are the head centre, which is receptive to impression from higher sources, and the ajna centre which is the recipient of the idealistic intuitional impressions; this ajna centre can then "broadcast" that which is received and recognised, using the throat centre as the creative formulator of thought, and the factor which embodies the sensed or intuited idea.

It will be apparent to you, therefore, how necessary it is to have a better recognition of the activity of the centres, as they are detailed in the Hindu philosophy; and until there is some real understanding of the part the vital body plays as the broadcaster and as the recipient of feelings, thoughts and ideas, there will be little progress made in the right understanding of modes of communication.

There is an interesting parallel between the three modes of telepathic work and their three techniques of accomplishment, and the three major ways of communicating on Earth:

Instinctual telepathy.......train travel, stations everywhere.......telegraph
Mental telepathy..ocean travel, ports on the periphery of all lands..telephone
Intuitional telepathy.............air travel, landing place.............radio

That which is going on in connection with the human consciousness is ever externalised or finds its analogy upon the physical plane, and so it is in connection with developed sensitivity to impression.

There is still another way in which we can look at the entire subject of response between broadcasting areas of

---

* *Discipleship in the New Age*, I. Page 87.

consciousness and the receiving areas of consciousness. We might list the divisions of this process. Much must remain theoretical, and little can, as yet, be worked out in practice. However, let me list the various forms of telepathic work for your general instruction:

1. Telepathic work from *solar plexus to solar plexus.* With this we have already dealt. This is closely connected with feeling, and little or no thought is involved; it concerns emotions (fear, hate, disgust, love, desire and many other purely astral reactions). It is carried on instinctively and below the diaphragm.

2. Telepathic work from *mind to mind.* This is beginning to be possible, and many more people are capable of this kind of communication than is now realised. People today do not know whence various mental impressions come, and this greatly enhances the complexity of life at this time and increases the mental problem of thousands.

3. Telepathic work from *heart to heart.* This type of impression is the sublimation of the "feeling" response registered earlier upon the ladder of evolution in the solar plexus. It concerns *only* group impressions, and is the basis of the condition spoken of in the Bible in connection with the greatest *Sensitive* humanity has ever produced, the Christ. There He is referred to as "A man of sorrows and acquainted with grief," but in this condition no *personal* sorrow or grief is involved. It is simply the consciousness of the sorrow of the world and the weight of grief under which humanity struggles. "The fellowship of Christ's suffering" is the reaction of the disciple to the same world condition. This is the true "broken heart," and is as yet a very rare thing to find. The usual broken heart is literally a disrupted solar plexus centre, bringing complete demolition of what is occultly called "the centre of feeling," and consequently the wrecking of the nervous system. It is

really brought about by a failure to handle conditions as a soul.

4. Telepathic work from *soul to soul*. This is, for humanity, the highest possible type of work. When a man can begin, as a soul, to respond to other souls and their impacts and impressions, then he is rapidly becoming ready for the processes which lead to initiation.

There are two other groups of telepathic possibilities which I would like to list for you. They are possibilities only when the four above-mentioned groups of telepathic impression are beginning to form a conscious part of the disciple's experience.

5. Telepathic work between *soul and mind*. This is the technique whereby the mind is "held steady in the light," and then becomes aware of the content of the soul's consciousness, an innate content, or that which is part of the group life of the soul on its own level, and when in telepathic communication with other souls, as mentioned under our fourth heading. This is the true meaning of intuitional telepathy. Through this means of communication the mind of the disciple is fertilised with the new and spiritual ideas; he becomes aware of the great Plan; his intuition is awakened. One point should here be borne in mind, which is oft forgotten: The inflow of the new ideas from the buddhic levels, thus awakening the intuitional aspect of the disciple, indicates that his soul is beginning to integrate consciously and definitely with the Spiritual Triad, and therefore to identify itself less and less with the lower reflection, the personality. This mental sensitivity and rapport between soul and mind remain for a long time relatively inchoate on the mental plane. That which is sensed remains too vague or too abstract for formulation. It is the stage of the mystical vision and of mystical unfoldment.

6. Telepathic work between *soul, mind and brain*. In

this stage the mind still remains the recipient of impression from the soul but, in its turn, it becomes a "transmitting agent" or communicator. The impressions received from the soul, and the intuitions registered as coming from the Spiritual Triad, via the soul, are now formulated into thoughts; the vague ideas and the vision hitherto unexpressed can now be clothed in form and sent out as embodied thoughtforms to the brain of the disciple. In time, and as the result of technical training, the disciple can in this way reach the mind and brains of other disciples. This is an exceedingly interesting stage. It constitutes one of the major rewards of right meditation and involves much true responsibility. You will find more anent this stage of telepathy in my other books, particularly *A Treatise on White Magic*.*

This much that I have outlined here is practically all that concerns man in his own inner individual contacts and work and training. There is, however, a whole range of telepathic contacts which should be noted because they constitute the goal for humanity.

7. Telepathic work between *a Master (the focal point of a group) and the disciple in the world*. It is an occult truth that no man is really admitted into a Master's group, as an accepted disciple, until he has become spiritually impressionable and can function as a mind in collaboration with his own soul. Prior to that he cannot be a conscious part of a functioning group on the inner planes gathered around a personalised force, the Master; he cannot work in true rapport with his fellow disciples. But when he can work somewhat as a conscious soul, then the Master can begin to impress him with group ideas via his own soul. He hovers then for quite a while upon the periphery of the group. Eventually, as his spiritual sensitivity increases, he

---

* Pages 176-180, 415, 427-428, 477-478.

can be definitely impressed by the Master and taught the technique of contact. Later, the group of disciples, functioning as one synthetic thoughtform, can reach him and thus automatically he becomes one of them. To those who have the true esoteric sense, the above paragraph will convey a good deal of information, hitherto hidden.

8. Telepathic work between *a Master and His group*. This is the mode of work whereby a Master trains and works through His disciples. He impresses them *simultaneously* with an idea or an aspect of truth. By watching their reactions, He can gauge the united activity of the group and the simultaneity of their response.

9. Telepathic work between *subjective and objective groups*. I do not refer here to the contact between an inner group of disciples, functioning consciously on the subjective levels, and the outer form that group takes. I refer to an inner group and a different outer group or groups. These groups, on both levels, can be either good or bad, according to the quality or calibre of the group personnel and their motives. This opens up a wide range of contacts and is one of the ways in which the Hierarchy of Masters work, as individuals. It is, however, not possible for groups upon the outer plane to respond to this type of contact until the bulk of their members have the heart centre awakened. In this connection a most interesting point should be noted. The awakening of the heart centre indicates inclusiveness, group appreciation and contact, also group thought and group life-activity. Unless, however, the head centre is also awakened and active, the soul is not able to control, and this heart activity need not necessarily be what we call good or spiritual activity. It is quite impersonal, like the sun, of which the heart is, as you know, the symbol. It shines alike upon the good and the bad; and group activity, as a result of heart awakening, can include the bad groups

as well as the good groups. Therefore you can see the necessity of awakening the head centre and bringing in the control of the soul aspect; and hence the emphasis laid upon character building and the need for meditation.

10. Telepathic work between *the Hierarchy of Masters as a group or a part of the Hierarchy, and groups of disciples*. There is little I can tell you about this, and you would not and could not understand. The experiment we are now making, in connection with the New Group of World Servers, is related to this form of telepathic work.

Some of these forms of telepathic work have necessarily their distorted reflections on the physical plane. These you might like to ponder upon, and trace the correspondences between them. What is "mass psychology" with its unreasoning quality and its blind activity, but a massed reaction to solar plexus impressions as passed from group to group? What is "public opinion," so called, but vague mental reactions by the mass of men beginning to grope their way on the mental plane, to the activity and play of more active and powerful minds? The written and spoken words are not in themselves adequate to account for the display of modern opinion as we now have it. What is the apparently accurate information, so rapidly circulated among the savage races, but an expression of that instinctual telepathy which uses the vital body and the pranic fluids as its medium?

Telepathic inter-relation between the members of a group grows through the medium of a constant attitude of reflective thought and a steadfast love for each other. I would remind you that when I use these terms I am referring to the two major types of energy in the world today. Essentially, energy is active substance. These two types of force are of a vitality, potency and substance so subtle and fine that they can work through and "force into activity" the pranic fluids which constitute the substance of the etheric body and to which I referred in a much earlier instruction.* The telepathic work, therefore, is concerned with three types of energy which demonstrate as forces with the power to motivate:

1. The *force of love* with its negative quality which

    a. Attracts the needed material with which to clothe the idea, the thought or concept to be transmitted; it is also the *attractive* agency utilised by the recipient. Therefore both transmitter and recipient work with the same agency, but the transmitter uses the love energy of the larger whole whilst the recipient concentrates, upon the transmitter, the love energy of his own nature. If this be so, you can see why I emphasise the necessity for love and for non-criticism.

    b. Constitutes the coherent quality which links together the transmitter and the recipient, and which also produces the coherency of that which is transmitted.

---

* *A Treatise on the Seven Rays,* II, 113.

It will be apparent to you consequently that it is only at this time that we can begin to look for a wider and more general expression in the world today of the processes of telepathy, for only today is the love principle really beginning to affect the world on a large scale. Love of a cause, a party or an idea is becoming more and more prevalent, producing in the initial stages the apparently wide cleavages with which we are so familiar and by which we are so distressed at this time, yet producing finally a dominance of the attitudes of love which will heal breaches, and produce synthesis among the peoples. *Love (not sentiment) is the clue to successful telepathic work.* Therefore love one another with a fresh enthusiasm and devotion; seek to express that love in every possible way—upon the physical plane, upon the levels of emotion, and through right thought. Let the love of the soul sweep through all like a regenerating force.

2. The *force of mind.* This is the illuminating energy which "lights the way" of an idea or form to be transmitted and received. Forget not that light is subtle substance. Upon a beam of light can the energy of the mind materialise. This is one of the most important statements made in connection with the science of telepathy.

The success of this is dependent upon the alignment of the bodies of the transmitter and the recipient. The double line of contact must be that of mental energy and brain electrical energy. The magnetic power of love to attract attention, to produce alignment, and to call forth rapport and understanding is not all that is necessary in the new telepathy which will distinguish the new age. There must also be mental development and mental control.

This form of telepathy is not a function of the animal soul, as in the case of the solar plexus contact and response to messages by the emotionally polarised man or woman. This telepathic rapport and response is a characteristic of the human soul working from mind to mind and from brain to brain. It is literally a state of consciousness which is sufficiently conditioned by the integrated mental person so that he is aware of and inclusive of the mental state and thought processes of another person.

3. The *energy of prana,* or the etheric force of the vital body. This energy, by an act of the will and under the pressure of the magnetic power of love, responds to or is receptive to the dual energies mentioned above. The idea, thoughtform or mental impression which must be recorded in the brain consciousness of the recipient opens a way in the pranic fluids and so controls their activity (which is as ceaseless as the thoughtform-making propensities of the *chitta*) that the brain becomes responsive in two ways:

   a. It is rendered passive by the impact of the three types of energy, blended and fused into one stream of force.

   b. It becomes actively responsive to the idea, impression, thoughtform, symbol, words, etc., which are being swept into the area of its conscious activity.

Let me attempt to reduce the above information to practical simplicity, thus showing how these three types of energy can be used in practical work:

1. By the use of *the energy of love* in three ways:

   a. By sending out love (not sentiment) to your brothers at the time of transmission or reception.

b. By capitalising on the inherent power of love to attract the material or the substance, and thus to "clothe" in the occult sense that which you send out.

c. By sending forth the "clothed" idea, impression, etc., on a stream of love which your brother—alert, receptive and waiting—will attract to himself by the means of his conscious love for you.

2. By the use of *mental energy* through the effort to polarise yourself upon the mental levels of consciousness. By a definite act of the will you lift your consciousness onto the mental plane and hold it there. This action is a reflection upon a lower plane, and *in the brain consciousness,* of the mind's ability to hold itself in the light. The success of all telepathic work you do, as a group or as individuals, will be dependent upon your capacity to "hold yourselves steady in the light" mentally. The difference is that this time you do it for the purpose of the planned work, and attempt to hold the mind steady in the light of the group, or in each other's light, and not so specifically in the light of your own soul.

3. By the conscious organised use of the energy of *the etheric ajna centre,* and sometimes of the head centre, when receiving, and of the throat centre, when transmitting. This swings etheric force into activity when engaged in telepathic work, but entails its conscious subordination to the power of the other two energies. Practically, you will observe that this involves on the part of the disciple the power to do three things at once. You need to ponder more deeply upon the fact and necessity of active outgoing energy

when you are occupied with the task of transmission, and with active receptivity when you are functioning as a receiver.

I would like to point out that successful telepathic work is dependent upon the following factors:

First, that there are no barriers existing between the receiver and the broadcaster. Such barriers would be lack of love or of sympathy, criticism and suspicion.

Secondly, that the broadcaster is mainly occupied with the clarity of his symbol, with the word or thought, and *not with the receiver*. A quick glance toward the receiver, a momentary sending forth of love and understanding is sufficient to set up the rapport, and then attention must be paid to the clarity of the symbol.

Thirdly, let the receivers think with love and affection of the broadcaster for a minute or two. Then let them forget the personality. A thread of energy, linking receiver and broadcaster, has been established and *exists*. Then forget it.

Fourthly, let the receivers work with detachment. Most receivers are so anxious to receive correctly that through their very intensity they counteract their own efforts. A casual and "don't care" spirit and a close attentiveness to the inner "picturing faculty" will net better results than any violent and strong desire and effort to see the symbol and to contact the mind of the sender.

The brain should register a reflection of the mind content. If a ray of light is met by an outgoing force from the receiver's mind or a powerfully emitted thoughtform, it can be prevented from reaching the mind. However, a transmitter with more expert training can overcome this barrier. Much of the trouble will be found to be based on the emitted thoughtforms, or in the rush of ill-regulated mental energy or brain radiation which negates efforts. Therefore a quiet spirit and well regulated thoughts will aid much, and the cultivation of that dispassion which desires nothing for the separated self, and nothing violently.

The need of sensitive receivers is great. Train yourselves. Forget yourselves and your own petty little affairs—so petty and unimportant when viewed in relation to the momentous issues of the present time. Keep an attentive ear to the voices which issue forth from the world of spiritual Being, and love each other with loyalty and steadfastness.

I would like to point out that the use of words tele-pathically must be mastered as a preliminary step to the use of sentences and of thoughts. Choose a word and medi-tate upon it, knowing wherefore you have chosen it. Study it in the four ways indicated by Patanjali; * that is:

1. Study its form, study it symbolically, as a word picture.
2. Study it from the angle of quality, of beauty, of desire.
3. Study its underlying purpose and teaching value, and its mental appeal.
4. Study its very being and identify yourself with its divine underlying idea.

When you have reached this final stage, hold your conscious-ness steady at that high point as you (if you are a trans-mitter) send out the word to the receiver or to the receiving group. Receivers should in their turn achieve, as far as they can, complete alignment so as to be responsive to all these four aspects of the word. This method will serve to shift the receiver nearer to the plane where he should function— the level of the higher mind. The word goes out upon the life breath of the transmitter; his lower mind then sends out the purpose aspect; his astral consciousness is respon-sible for sending out the quality aspect; and the form aspect is sent out as he *says* the word—very softly and in a whisper.

The above is a good exercise and very simple; telepathic power should greatly increase if one faithfully follows these four stages—up and within, down and without—in the

---

* *The Light of the Soul,* page 33.

work of transmitting. During the first or form stage one may use what symbolic forms one likes to embody the word, for such a word as "will" has no appropriate form like "pool" has; one may, if he choose, preserve the word form, seeing it letter for letter or as a whole. But one must be sure to end with the picture form or the word form with which he began; and that he sends out, at the close, what he formulated at the beginning.

To summarise: A group of disciples working in an Ashram has to learn that—

1. Groups are held together by an inner structure of thought.

2. The focus of the externalised group life is the etheric body.

The etheric body is:
   a. A receiving agency.
   b. A circulating medium for energy coming from the mind, from the soul, from the Master, or from the group mind.

3. The mind is the first exoteric expression of the soul consciousness, as far as the true aspirant is concerned.

4. The following telepathic relationships are possible and must be borne in mind:
   a. Solar plexus to solar plexus.
   b. Mind to mind.
   c. Master to disciple.
   d. Groups of disciples to other similar groups.
   e. Subjective groups to objective receptive groups.
   f. The Hierarchy, through its great Leaders, to the various Ashrams of the Masters.

g. The Hierarchy to the New Group of World Servers.

5. The major factors which must be considered in all telepathic work are:
   a. The initiating agent or emanating source.
   b. The recipient of the ideas, thoughts or energy.
   c. The medium of revelation.

The growth of telepathic rapport will bring in an era of universality and synthesis, with its qualities of recognised relationships and responsiveness. This will be, outstandingly, the glory of the Aquarian Age.

As the race achieves increasingly a mental polarisation through the developing attractive power of the mental principle, the use of language for the *conveying of thoughts between equals or of communicating with superiors* will fall into disuse. It will continue to be used in reaching the masses and those not functioning upon the mental plane. Already voiceless prayer and aspiration and worship are deemed of higher value than the pleadings and proclamations of voiced expression. It is for this stage in the unfoldment of the race for which preparation must be made, and the laws, techniques and process of telepathic communication must be made plain so that they can be intelligently and theoretically understood.

Disciples must occupy themselves increasingly with right understanding, right designation and right definition of the new science of telepathy. Mental comprehension and mental sympathy will make true interplay possible, and this will bridge between the old way of understanding thought through the medium of the spoken or written word (embodying that thought as the individual thinker seeks to convey it) and the future stage of immediate response to thought, unlimited by speech or other medium of expression. Disciples will endeavour to work in both ways, and the medium of normal human relations and that of super-normal subjective relations must be studied by them and expressed by them. In this way the time of bridging and the period of transition can be spanned. It will take about five hundred years for the race to become normally telepathic, and when I say normally I mean *consciously*. This bridging work must be carried forward by disciples in three ways:

1. By an endeavour to understand:

    a. The medium of transmission.

    b. The method of transmission.

    c. The manner of reception.

    d. The mode of inter-related activity.

2. By the cultivation of sensitive reactions to each other and to the other human units with whom the lot of the disciples may be cast. This involves:

    a. Sensitive physical reaction, via the centres, to the forces emanating from the centres of those with whom the disciples are associated. Particularly should the sensitivity of the ajna centre be developed.

    b. Sensitivity to the state of feeling or to the emotional reactions of those around. This is done through the development of compassion and of sympathy, plus that detachment which will enable one to take right action.

    c. Sensitivity to the thoughts of others through mental rapport with them upon the plane of mind.

3. By all these done also in group formation as well as individually. All the activities mentioned above must constitute *group activity*.

In these three ways the vehicle of the personality can be so conditioned that it can become a sensitive receiving apparatus. When, however, soul consciousness is achieved or developing, then this triple instrument is superseded by the intuitional receptivity of the soul—whose inclusiveness is absolute and who is at-one with the soul in all forms.

Those disciples who are working along this line are the nurturers of the seed of the future intuitional civilisation, which will come to its full glory in the Aquarian Age. The intuition is the infallibly sensitive agent, latent in every human being; it is based, as you know, upon direct knowledge, unimpeded by any instrument normally functioning in the three worlds. Of this intuitional future age, Christ is the *Seed Man,* for "He knew what was in man." Today, a group or a unit of groups can be the nurturers of the seed of the intuition; the cultivation of sensitivity to telepathic impression is one of the most potent agencies in developing the coming use of the intuitive faculty.

The truly telepathic man is the man who is responsive to impressions coming to him from all forms of life in the three worlds, but he is also equally responsive to impressions coming to him from the world of souls and the world of the intuition. It is the development of the telepathic instinct which will eventually make a man a master in the three worlds, and also in the five worlds of human and super-human development. By a process of withdrawal (of occult abstraction) and of concentration upon the telepathic cult, the whole science of telepathy (as a seed of a future racial potency) can be developed and understood. This is a process now going forward, and it is going on in two ways:

through the medium of telepathic groups and of telepathic people, and through the medium of exoteric scientific investigation. The building of the thoughtform which will accustom the race to the idea of telepathic work is proceeding apace, and the seed of this development is becoming very vital and powerful and germinating with real rapidity. It is, in the last analysis, the seed of MASTERHOOD.

I shall now take up with you the subject of *united* group telepathic work, its possibilities and the present opportunity, touching upon the dangers involved and the responsibility which will rest upon your shoulders and upon those of all disciples who may attempt to work in this way. You need to bear in mind the following three injunctions:

First: It is essential that you acquire *facility* in tuning in on each other with deepest love and understanding; that you develop *impersonality* so that when a brother tunes in on a weakness or a strength, upon a mistake or a right attitude, it evokes from you no slightest reaction that could upset the harmony of the group united work as planned; that you cultivate a *love* which will ever seek to strengthen and to help, and a power to supplement or complement each other which will be of use in balancing the group, as a working unit under spiritual impression. The discovery of a weakness in a group brother should only produce the evocation of a deeper love; the discovery that you have made a mistake (if you have) in interpreting a brother should only prompt you to a renewed vital effort to approach more closely to his soul; the revelation to you of a brother's strength will indicate where you can look for help in any hour of your own need. State frankly what you feel as you work month after month at this task of group rapport, deliberately tuning out criticism and substituting for it analysis—an analysis impersonally given; state truthfully what you sense and register. Your conclusions may be right or wrong, but a definite effort to comply and to recognise consciously the gained impression should aid the group blending without undue delay into an instrument of sensitive understanding. If disciples cannot tune in on each other

37

with ease after long periods of close relationship, how can
they, as a group, tune in on some individual or some group
of individuals unknown to them in their personalities? Unless such interplay is established fundamentally and unless
there is a close integration between the members who constitute the group, it will not be possible for constructively
useful and spiritually oriented and controlled work to be
properly carried forward and successfully accomplished.
But it is a task which you can accomplish if you will, and
real application over a period of time should enable the
group to work smoothly and well together. The three
Rules * for beginners, earlier given, embody the first steps
leading to the attitude required in true hierarchical work;
this is the objective of the accepted disciple.

Secondly: Your constant effort—to be carried forward
steadily and slowly—must be to bring about a *group love*
of such strength that nothing can break it and no barriers
rise up between you; to cultivate a *group sensitivity* of such
a quality that your diagnosis of conditions will be relatively
accurate; to develop and unfold a *group ability to work as
a unit,* so that there will be nothing in the inner attitudes
of any of the group members which could break into the
carefully established rhythm. For it is quite possible for a
member of the group to retard the work and to hold back
the group because he is so engrossed in his own affairs or
in his own ideas of self-development; when some members
cease their activity it does affect the inner group vibration;
when others become slowed up by definite changes in their
outer or inner lives, this requires periods of adjustment
and oft of re-organisation of the life. These changes, being
externalised, can produce powerful psychological changes
and upset the rhythm of the soul's endeavour. A tried and

* *A Treatise on White Magic,* page 320.

experienced disciple will not let such a change upset his inner rhythm, but a less experienced disciple needs real soul watchfulness to the danger of sidetracking the life interest from spiritual purposes to personality attentions and interests.

Thirdly: Any group work of this kind must be most carefully controlled; any group effort which seeks to impress the mind of any subject (whether an individual or a group) must be strenuously guarded as to motive and method; any group endeavour which involves a united applied effort to effect changes in the point of view, an outlook on life, or a technique of living must be *utterly selfless,* most wisely and cautiously undertaken, and must be kept free from any personality emphasis, any personality pressure and any mental pressure which is formulated in terms of individual belief, prejudice, dogmatism or ideas. I would ask you to study the above few words most carefully.

The moment that there is the least tendency on the part of a group, or of an individual in a group, to force an issue, to bring so much mental pressure to bear that an individual or group is helpless under the impact of other minds, you have what is called "black magic." Right motive may protect the group from any serious results to themselves, but the effect upon their victim will be definitely serious, rendering him negative, and with a weakened will.

The result of all *true* telepathic work and rightly directed effort to "impress" a subject will be to leave him with a strengthened will to right action, an intensified interior light, an astral body freer from glamour, and a physical body more vital and purer. The potency of a united group activity is incredibly powerful. The occult aphorism that "energy follows thought" is either a statement of a truth or else a meaningless phrase.

Forget not that the method of work of the Hierarchy is that of *impression* upon the minds of Their disciples, of telepathic work carried on with the Master as broadcaster and the disciple as the recipient of impression and of energy. This reception of impression and energy has a dual effect:

1. It brings into activity the latent seeds of action and of habits (good or bad), thus producing revelation, purification, enrichment and usefulness.
2. It vitalises and galvanises the personality into a right relation to the soul, to the environment, and to humanity.

It is necessary for you and for all disciples to grasp the correspondence to this hierarchical effort and any effort which you may make in order to work as a group of individuals with groups or individuals. An appreciation of the power which you may let loose, of the dynamic effect which you may succeed in awakening in the subject of your directed thought, and of the impression which you may imprint in the mind and consciousness of the subject should incite you to a guarded purity of life (astral and physical), to a watchfulness over thoughts and ideas, and to a love which will safeguard you from all love of power. Thus you will preserve the integrity of those you seek to help and will be enabled to suggest, to strengthen and to teach subjectively with no undue influence, no forcing, and no infringement of the liberty and spiritual franchise of the person concerned. A difficult task, my brothers, but one to which you are equal, given due attention and obedience to the above three injunctions as to motive, technique and method.

The entire subject of telepathic communication can be approached under a more subjective designation or name, but one which is interpretive of the more universal and prior stage than that of direct telepathic reception. The occultist ever approaches the subject connected with the evolutionary process from the angle of the whole and then the part, from the periphery to the centre, from the universal to the particular. Among Themselves, the Masters do not deal with telepathy as a science warranting consideration, endeavour and impartation; They are concerned primarily with the *Science of Impression*. The term most often employed by Them is the esoteric equivalent of what the average person means when he says, "I have an impression." Impression is the subtlest reaction (more or less accurate) to the vibratory mental activity of some other mind or group of minds, of some whole, as its radiatory influence affects the unit or aggregate of units.

The first stage of correct telepathic reception is ever the registering of an impression; it is generally vague at the beginning, but as a thought, idea, purpose or intention of the sending agent concretises, it slips into the second stage which appears as a definite thoughtform; finally, that thoughtform makes its impact upon the consciousness of the brain in the location lying just behind the ajna centre and consequently in the area of the pituitary body. It can appear also in the region of the solar plexus centre. But for those Lives Who have surmounted life in the three worlds and Who are not conditioned by the triple mechanism of the personality, *the impression* is the factor of importance; Their consciousness is impressed, and so sensitive is Their response to the higher impression, that They absorb or appropriate the impression so that it becomes a part of Their own "impulsive energy."

This is by no means an easy subject for me to elucidate, and the reasons are two:

1. The members of the Hierarchy (among Whom I have the status of Master)* are Themselves in process of learning this Science of Impression. This They do on the levels of the abstract mind, of the intuition, or of manas and buddhi.

2. The science is as yet without a vocabulary. It is not limited at any stage by thoughtforms but it is limited by word forms; and it is therefore a difficult problem for me to pass on any information anent this subtle mode of communication of which telepathy is in fact but an exoteric externalisation.

Impression, as an art to be mastered both from the angle of the impressing agent and of the impressed recipient, is definitely related to the world of ideas. As far as our planetary Life is concerned, there are certain great sources of impression and one or two of them might here be noted; you will thus gain some idea of the subtlety of the whole subject, of its close relation to energy impacts and of its group reception as differentiated from individual reception, as is the case in any telepathic rapport.

1. *The impression of Shamballa* by:

   a. Members of the Great White Lodge on Sirius. The recipients of this impression are the highest Members of the Great Council, presided over by the Lord of the World. So subtle is this im-

---

* *Discipleship in the New Age*, I, **777**.

pression that these Great Lives can only receive it with accuracy when in full joint conference of the entire Council, and also after due preparation.

b. From one or other of the constellations which are at any particular time astrologically en rapport with our planet. This impression can only be received by the Great Council when sitting in conclave with a majority of its Members present. This, I would have you note, does not entail the attendance of the entire Council.

c. From a triangle of circulating energy, emanating from the two planets which—with our planet, the Earth—form a triangle in any particular cycle. This impression is received by the three Buddhas of Activity for distribution to the Hierarchy.

d. From the planet Venus, the Earth's *alter ego*. This makes its entrance via the Lord of the World and three of His Council Who are chosen by Him at any specific time to act as recipients.

These are the major entering impressions, recorded by what is glibly called "the Universal Mind," the mind of God, our planetary Logos. There are other entering impressions, but to them I do not refer, as any reference would be meanngless to you.

2. *The impression of the Hierarchy* by:

a. Shamballa itself through the medium of groups within the Great Council; these step down the impression which they register so that the Hierarchy—as a whole—may cooperate with the purposes intended by those who are forming the needed Plan.

b. Certain great Lives Who, at specific times and according to cyclic rhythm, or in times of emergency, are swung into this type of activity. For instance, one such time would be the Full Moon period, which is a time of reception by the Hierarchy as well as by Humanity; an instance of the second type of activity would be the Wesak Festival, or those acute crises when intervention is required from sources far higher than those with which the recipient is usually en rapport. Such a crisis is fast approaching.

The first type of impression is rhythmic, recurrent and therefore cumulative in its intended effects. The second type of impression is the result of invocation and evocation and is dependent upon both the recipient and the agent.

c. That great group of divine Contemplatives who are trained to act as an intermediate receptive group between Shamballa and the Hierarchy. They receive impression from Shamballa and transmit it to the Hierarchy, thus enabling the Members of the Hierarchy to receive it as "a sharpened impression" and to register it accurately because the emanating impression has passed through an area within the divine Mind where it is enhanced by the trained perception and the determined receptivity of this group. They are called, in the East, the divine Nirmanakayas. I only mention Their occult name so that you may learn to recognise Them when you meet reference to Them.

d. The Buddha at the time when the Wesak Festival is celebrated. He then acts as a focal point or as the "distributor of the impression"; He then has behind Him (little as you may realise it) the entire impressing force of the Buddhas of Activity Who are to Shamballa what the Nirmanakayas are to the Hierarchy.

Let me here interpolate a remark which may prove helpful and illuminating. We are dealing (as you will undoubtedly have noted) with the reception of impression by groups or by aggregations of groups composed of living Beings Who have Their own agents of distribution or impression. The entire evolutionary history of our planet is one of reception and of distribution, of a taking in and of a giving out. The key to humanity's trouble (focussing, as it has, in the economic troubles of the past two hundred years, and in the theological impasse of the orthodox churches) has been to take and not to give, to accept and not to share, to grasp and not to distribute. This is the breaking of the Law which has placed humanity in the position of guilt. The war is the dire penalty which humanity has had to pay for this great sin of separateness. Impressions from the Hierarchy have been received, distorted, misapplied and misinterpreted, and the task of the New Group of World Servers is to offset this evil. These Servers are to humanity what the Buddhas of Activity are to Shamballa, and the group of divine Contemplatives (the Nirmanakayas) are to the Hierarchy. It might be stated therefore that:

1. The Buddhas of Activity are Themselves impressed by the WILL of God as it energises the entire planetary life.

2. The Nirmanakayas are impressed by the LOVE of God as it demonstrates itself as the attractive force which impulses the Plan inspired by the Purpose. In other words, it is the Hierarchy, impelled to action

by Shamballa, or the Will-to-Good, externalising itself as goodwill.

3. The New Group of World Servers are impressed by
the active INTELLIGENCE of God; they translate
this divine impression and step it down in two great
stages, therefore, bringing it into concrete manifestation.

We now carry this conception of divine impression down to
the level of the human consciousness.

3. *The impression of Humanity* by:

a. The Hierarchy, through the stimulating of ideas.
These demonstrate through a steadily growing
and enlightened public opinion.

b. The influence of the Ashrams of the Masters as
they affect the aspirants of the world, the humanitarians and the idealists. These impressing agencies, being seven in number, constitute seven
different streams of impressing energy which
affect the seven ray types. The united Ashrams,
forming the great Ashram of the Christ, affect
humanity as a whole; this great united Ashram
works solely through the New Group of World
Servers whose members are on all rays, of all
grades of development, and who work in all the
various departments of human living and enter-
prise.

c. The activity of the New Group of World Servers
about which I have already written in my various
pamphlets; therefore repetition is not necessary.*

It will be obvious to you that I have only touched upon a few,
a very few, of the impressing forces of the planet, and have

---

* *A Treatise on the Seven Rays,* II, 629-751. *A Treatise on White
Magic,* 398-433.

enumerated only a few of the major groups which are—in their intrinsic nature—both recipients of impression and a- gents later of the impressing agent. When we arrive at the human family, this reciprocal activity is blocked by human selfishness; it is this "interruption of impression" and this "interference with the divine circulatory flow" which (as I have said above) is responsible for sin, for disease, and for all the various factors which make humanity today what it is. When the free flow of divine energy, of divine interplay and of spiritual purpose is re-established, then evil will disappear and the will-to-good will become factual goodwill upon the outer physical plane.

In the statements given above in connection with the three great planetary centres you have the basis for the new and coming Approach to Divinity which will be known under the expression: Invocative and Evocative religion. It is this new Science of Impression which forms the subjective basis and the uniting element which binds together the en- tire realm of knowledge, of science and of religion. The fundamental ideas which underlie these great areas of human thought all emanate from intuitional levels; they finally condition the human consciousness, evoking man's aspiration to penetrate deeper into the arcana of all wisdom, for which knowledge is the preparatory stage. This Science of Impression is the mode of life of the subjective world which lies between the world of external happenings (the world of appearances and of exoteric manifestation) and the inner world of reality. This is a point which should be most carefully taken into the calculations of the occult investigators. Impressions are received and registered; they form the basis of reflection for those aspirants who are sensitive enough to their impact and wise enough to record carefully in consciousness their emanating source. After due practice, this period of brooding upon the registered impression is followed by another period wherein the impression begins to take form as an idea; from that point it follows the familiar course of translation from an idea into a presented ideal; it then comes under the invocative appeal of the more concrete-minded until it finally precipitates itself into outer manifestation and takes form. You will see, therefore, that what I am doing is to take the student a step further into the world of reception and perception and point him to the more subtle contacts which lie behind those concepts which are regarded as definitely nebulous and to which we give the name of intuitions.

The Science of Impression—if studied by the disciples in the world and by the New Group of World Servers—will greatly facilitate the presentation of those ideals which must and will condition the thinking of the New Age and will eventually produce the new culture and the new civilised expression which lies ahead of humanity, superseding the present civilisation and providing the next field of expression for mankind. This science is, in fact, the basis of the theory of relationships and will lead to the expansion of the idea of right human relations which has hitherto—as a phrase—been confined to an ideal desire for correct interplay between man and man, group and group, and nation and nation; it has also hitherto been restricted to the human society and interplay, and remains as yet a hope and a wish. When, however, the Science of Impression has been correctly apprehended and has been brought down to the level of an educational objective, it will be found to be closely linked to the emerging teaching anent invocation and evocation and will be expanded to include not only right human relations to the superhuman kingdoms, but right human relations with the subhuman kingdoms also. It will, therefore, be concerned with the sensitive response of the entire natural and supernatural world to the "One in Whom we live and move and have our being"; it will put mankind into a right relationship with all aspects and expressions of the divine nature, deepening subjective contact and bringing about a diviner objective manifestation and one more in line with divine purpose. It will lead to a great shift of the human consciousness off the levels of emotional and physical life (where the bulk of humanity is focussed) on to the levels of mental perception.

You will understand, consequently, the reason why the Knowers of the world have ever referred to the dual action of the mind as it is sensitive to the higher impressions and active in the mental creation of the needed thoughtforms. The mind, rightly trained, will seize upon the fugitive impression, subject it to the concretising effect of mental activity, produce the required form, and this, when correctly created and oriented, will finally lead to the externalising of the registered impression, as it took form in an intuition and eventually found its place upon the mental plane. You will see also why disciples and world workers have to function as MINDS, as receptive and perceptive intelligences and as creators in mental matter. It is all related to this Science of Impression with which we have been dealing. You will note also that this whole process is capable of expansion in the processes of meditation, so that the aspirant can be sensitive to impression and (because he is oriented to the world of ideas and is aware of the subtlety and delicacy of the apparatus required to register the "overshadowing cloud of knowable things") is safeguarded from the sensitivity required to register impacts from other minds, good or bad in their orientation, and from the thought currents of that which is in process of taking form as well as from the powerful pull or urge of the emotional and desire reactions of the astral plane and of the emotionally polarised world in which he lives physically.

More understanding will come also if you grasp the fact that this Science of Impression is concerned with the activity of the head centre as an anchoring centre for the antahkarana, and that the ajna centre is concerned with the process of translating the recorded intuition into a form (through recognition of and reaction to a mental thought-form) and its subsequent direction, as an ideal objective, into the world of men. In the early stages and until the third initiation, the Science of Impression is concerned with the establishing of a sensitivity (an invocative sensitivity) between the Spiritual Triad (temporarily expressing itself through the abstract mind and the soul or the Son of Mind) and the concrete mind. This mental triangle is a reflection, in time and space, of the Monad and of the two higher aspects of the Triad, and is reflected (after the process of invocation and a succeeding process of evocation) in another triad—that of the lower mind, the soul and the vital body. When the relation between the lower and the higher mind is correctly and stably established, you have the swinging into activity of the lowest triad connected with the Science of Impression—the head centre, the ajna centre and the throat centre.

In the above I have given you an interesting and brief elucidation of the technique to be applied to the energising of the centres in the human body. I would remind you that what is true of the individual disciple must be and is true of that great disciple—Humanity, the entire human family. It is also true, as an outgrowth of this idea, of all the three planetary centres: Shamballa, the Hierarchy and Humanity. The name *Science of Impression* is that given to the process whereby the establishment of the required relationship in all these units of life takes place. The *Technique of Invocation and Evocation* is the name given to the mode or method whereby the desired relationship is brought about.

The *Creative Work* is the name given to the manifestation of the results of the two above processes. The three aspects of the Technique of Invocation and Evocation with which the average disciple should concern himself are those of the building of the antahkarana, the correct use of the lower mind in its two higher functions (the holding of the mind steady in the light and the creation of the desired thoughtforms), and the process of precipitation whereby the impression is enabled eventually to take tangible form.

In the above exegesis I have given you much food for thought in connection with telepathic possibilities; it all fits into the theme of world service as it is to be applied in the expansion of the human consciousness on a large scale. This is one of the major tasks of the New Group of World Servers.

VIII. THE SUPREME SCIENCE OF CONTACT

It would be useful if you attempted to master and to assimilate what I have to impart anent the three great sciences which form the three modes of expression of what we might term the SUPREME SCIENCE OF CONTACT. These three sciences are all equally interdependent and all related to the art of responsiveness. They are:

1. The Science of Impression . . . . The will-to-be.
   Relation to the Spiritual Triad.
       Source of emanation . . . . Shamballa.
   Connected with the abstract mind.

2. The Science of Invocation and
   Evocation . . . . Love or attraction.
   Relation to the soul in all forms.
       Source of emanation (at this
       time) . . . . The Hierarchy.
   Connected with the lower
   mind, as the agent of the soul.

3. The Science of Telepathy. Mind. Human intelligence.
   Relation to the personality.
       Source of emanation . . . . Humanity itself.
   Connected with the head centre.

You will see how all these pairs of opposites play their part, exemplifying the dualistic nature of our planetary Life:

1. The abstract mind and the lower mind.
2. The soul and the lower mind.
3. The lower mind and the head centre.

Each of them acts as an invocative agent and produces evo-cation. All act as recipients and as transmitters, and all of them together establish the group inter-relation and the circulation of the energies which are the distinctive characteristic of the entire world of force.

One point you all need to grasp is that the progressing disciple does not move into new fields or areas of awareness, like a steady marching forward from one plane to another (as the visual symbols of the theosophical literature would indicate). What must be grasped is that *all that IS is ever present*. What we are concerned with is the constant awakening to that which eternally IS, and to what is ever present in the environment but of which the subject is un-aware, owing to short-sightedness. The aim must be to overcome the undue concentration upon the foreground of daily life which characterises most people, the intense pre-occupation with the interior states or moods of the lower self which characterises the spiritually minded people and the aspirants, and the imperviousness or lack of sensitivity which characterises the mass of men. The Kingdom of God is present on Earth today and forever has been, but only a few, relatively speaking, are aware of its signs and mani-festations. The world of subtle phenomena (called form-less, because unlike the physical phenomena with which we are so familiar) is ever with us and can be seen and con-tacted and proved as a field for experiment and experience and activity if the mechanism of perception is developed as it surely can be. The sounds and sights of the heavenly world (as the mystics call it) are as clearly perceived by the higher initiate as are the sights and sounds of the physical plane as you contact it in your daily round of duties. The world of energies, with its streams of directed force and its centres of concentrated light, is likewise present, and the eye of the see-er can see it, just as the eye of the mental clair-voyant can see the geometrical pattern which thoughts assume upon the mental plane, or as the lower psychic can contact the glamours, the illusions and delusions of the astral world. The subjective realm is vitally more real than is the objective, once it is entered and known. It is simply (how simple to some and how insuperably difficult to others, apparently!) a question of the acceptance, first of all, of its existence, the development of a mechanism of contact, the cultivation of the ability to use this mechanism at will, and then *inspired interpretation.*

It might be said that consciousness itself, which is the goal—on this planet—of all the evolutionary process, is simply the demonstrated result of the Science of Contact. It is likewise the goal in some form or other and at some stage or other of all planetary existences within the solar system itself. The unfoldment of this conscious response is, in reality, the growth of the sensitive awareness of the planetary Logos HIMSELF. The human mechanism and its ability to respond to its environment (as science well knows) has been developed in response to an inner urge, present in every human being and in all forms of life, and to the "pull" and magnetic effect of the surrounding environment. Step by step, the forms of life upon the physical plane, down through the ages, have unfolded one sense after another; one form of sensitive response after another becomes possible as the mechanism is produced, until the human being can receive impressions from the physical plane and rightly interpret them; can respond to the emotional contacts of the astral plane and succumb to them or surmount them; and can become telepathic to the world of the mental plane, thus sharing—physically, emotionally and mentally—in the life and contacts of the three worlds which constitute his environment and in which he is submerged whilst in incarnation. What he gets out of this life of constant impression is largely dependent upon his power to invoke his environment and draw from it (in evocative response) what he needs in all the various departments of his being. This, in its turn, forces him—whether he likes it or not—to produce an effect upon other people; this can be far more potent for good or evil, and from the telepathic angle, than he likes to think or can conceive. You see, therefore, how these sciences of Impression, of Invocation and Evocation, and of Telepathy are naturally concerned with what is inherent in man and in his relation to his environment and circumstances.

The germ **or** embryonic capacity for all types of planetary contact is inherent in every man and *will not be frustrated* in the long run. In this knowledge of goals already achieved in the three worlds lies the guarantee of achievement in the more subjective worlds which are present within the aspirant's surroundings but to which he remains as yet unawakened and unenlightened. I am seeking to make the matter as simple as I can, for much of the abstract formulations of the occult sciences and the academic psychologists are incident to the over-activity of men's minds and emotional natures. If you can grasp certain broad and relatively simple facts and recognise that you possess the key or the clue in your already developed capacities, then you will go forward with simplicity, making no undue intellectual difficulties when dealing with these more subtle phases of your ever-existent environment. It is, in the last analysis, just a question as to what "impresses" you at any given moment, and then in what manner it conditions you.

You will see, therefore, how much that I have already said links up with the teaching I have given upon the Points of Revelation. In the very condensed summation of the Science of Impression, I touched briefly upon the three great groups of Lives that are constantly under "impression" and which, in their turn, become "impressing agents." There is little that can be added to this theme with profit at this time; what has already been given should be studied and related to the teaching on the Points of Revelation.*

Revelation is a generic term covering all the responses to the activities of the eye of the mind, the eye of the soul, and the "insight" of the Universal Mind which contact with the Monad gives. Sight is the greatest of all the developments in this world period in which the Logos is seeking to bring the subhuman kingdoms to the point where *human* vision is theirs, to bring humanity to the point where *spiritual* vision is developed and hierarchical insight is the normal quality of the initiate sight, and to bring the Members of the Hierarchy to the point where *universal* perception is Theirs. Therefore, it might be said that:

1. *Through the door of individualisation* the subhuman kingdoms pass to human vision, leading to mental contact and intelligent impression.
2. *Through the door of initiation* humanity passes to spiritual vision, leading to soul contact and spiritual impression.
3. *Through the door of identification* the Hierarchy passes to universal vision, leading to monadic contact and extra-planetary impression.

Each time that there is a fresh vision of a compelling and conditioning nature, it is the result of invocation by the

* *Discipleship in the New Age,* Volume II, Section 3.

one seeking the new impression. When this invocative spirit is present, the results are inevitable and sure and the response evoked cannot be stopped. This is the basis of all the success of desire (material or otherwise), aspiration, prayer and meditation. Always we get—in time and space—what we invoke; and the knowledge of this fact, scientifically applied, will be one of the great liberating forces for humanity.

The training given by the Masters in Their Ashrams to Their disciples has one main objective: to increase, develop and enable them to utilise in service their inherent and innate sensitivity. Let us, as we discuss these matters, avoid that much over-worked word "vibration" and use instead the more simple and more easily understood word "impact". Response to impact is something we all register. Our five senses have opened to all people five great realms from which impact comes, and we are so familiar with them all that our response is now automatic and, though registered, is not consciously so, unless there is a planned reason and direction intended. We respond similarly and as automatically to emotional stimuli, and rapidly (very rapidly) the race is reaching out towards mental telepathy. Some few are beginning to work along the lines of spiritual telepathy. Few do more than register occasionally contacts emanating from a high source, and the result is usually also over-mixed with personality reactions.

Contact, with resultant impact from the soul, is also quite rapidly developing, hence the necessity for my laying the foundations of further knowledge which will clarify still higher contact, emanating from the Spiritual Triad and opening up areas of interaction hitherto known only to the Hierarchy. I refer here to the teaching which I have given out through a group of my disciples anent the Antahkarana.* All such developing contacts involve conditions covered by the two words: Contact and Impact.

---

* *Education in the New Age.*
  A Treatise on the Seven Rays, Volume V.

1. *Contact* can be defined (for our particular purposes) as recognition of an environment, an area of the hitherto unknown, of that which has somehow been evoked, of a something other which has made its presence felt. This something other than the Perceiver has usually been *earlier sensed*, has been propounded into a *theoretical possibility,* has later been *invoked* by the directed and conscious attention of the one who has sensed its presence, and finally *contact* is made.

2. *Impact* is something more than simply registering contact. It develops into conscious interaction; it conveys later information; it is revelatory in nature, and can be defined in its initial stages as the guarantee to the one who responds to it of a new area for exploration and for spiritual adventure, and as the indication of a wider field wherein consciousness may expand more and more and register increasingly the divine purpose waiting to be more fully known.

Therefore, from the more normal field of what we may call ordinary telepathic perception (just now coming to recognition by ordinary science), through a slowly learnt process of invocation and evocation, to a state of consciousness distinguished by a trained sensitivity, the disciple moves. He unfolds a spiritual recognition which is controlled, understood, and directed to useful hierarchical ends. In these words, you have a very simple definition of the process to which we give, technically, the name: The Science of Impression.

Another point to remember is that this science is the basic Science of Sensitivity; it is the art of all responsiveness to phenomena and is peculiarly applied to the reaction, the recognition, the responsiveness, and the registration of all phenomena to be found throughout the cosmic physical plane. This is the plane whereon our entire threefold planetary Life finds expression and which we have subdivided (for the sake of clear thinking) into the seven planes (so called) of our solar system—from what we call our lowest physical plane up to our highest plane, the logoic. In the earlier stages of responsiveness to the two phases of contact and impact, the first task is to develop the needed apparatus of contact, the medium of learning, the mechanism of registration, and then learning to use it constructively and intelligently. This work proceeds from cycle to cycle, in the earliest stages, with no conscious intention on the part of the unit of life, thus developing; yet field after field of consciousness is slowly recorded, and area after area of the surrounding physical, mental and spiritual worlds come within the arena of perception, and are mastered and controlled, until eventually the unit of life (I know not what else to call it) becomes the human being, self-directed, an individual. Finally the man becomes the Master, controlling and directing within the periphery of His wide awareness, in consonance with the divine Mind and Plan.

But—and this is a point I seek to impress upon you— humanity, subjected to this constant process of expansion from the emergence of the fourth kingdom in nature, the human, has now reached the stage where it can begin to pass out of the control of what has been called the Law of Triple Response into a new phase of unfoldment where a recognised dualism dominates. This is a most important statement. Let me word it in this way and let me commend to you a very careful consideration of my words. I will express what I seek to impart in certain short sentences and in tabulation form:

1. The advanced man in the three worlds is conscious of two inherent triplicities:
   a. The lower man ....Physical body.
   Astral nature.
   Mind.
   b. The three periodical vehicles ....Monad. Soul.
   Personality.
2. Soul and personality have made contact. He is now technically soul-infused. Two periodical vehicles have been at-oned. Three lower vehicles and the soul are united.
3. The etheric body is at the point of assuming great power. It can now be consciously used as a transmitter of:
   a. Energy and forces, consciously directed.
   b. Impacts from the highest of the periodical vehicles, working through its instrument, the Spiritual Triad.
4. The etheric body is, therefore, the agent consciously directed, of the rapidly integrating spiritual unity. It can convey into the brain the needed energies and that occult information which together make a man a Master of the Wisdom and eventually a Christ— all-inclusive in HIS developed attractive and magnetic power.

Elsewhere I made the following statement which, as you study it, will summarise the above detailed analysis. I said, defining impression, that it *"concerns the engendering of a magnetic aura on which the highest impressions can play."* This might also serve as a definition of the art of invocation and evocation. As the man (for we will not consider this science apart from him, as it would include too vast a field) becomes sensitive to his environment, as the forces of evo-

NOTE: See Chart *The Constitution of Man,* p. x.

lution play upon him and lead him on from stage to stage, from point to point, from plane to plane, and from height to height, he becomes enriched and increasingly magnetic. As this attractive or magnetic force increases, he himself becomes invocative; this outgoing demand, emanating from or through the aura which he has engendered brings to him a developing revelation. This revelation, in its turn, enriches the magnetic field of his aura so that he becomes a revealing centre to those whose field of experience and aura need the stimulus of his practiced assurance.

Finally, it might be said that the entire human kingdom will eventually be a major magnetic centre upon our planet, invoking all the higher kingdoms upon the formless planes and evoking all the lower or subhuman kingdoms upon the planes of form. Some day, two-thirds of the human family will be sensitive to impacts coming from the Mind of God, as that Mind fulfills its intentions and carries out its purposes within our planetary ring-pass-not. In its turn, humanity will provide the area of mind within whose ring-pass-not the subhuman kingdoms will find the correspondence of the Universal Mind which they need for their unfoldment; man, as you well know, is the macrocosm for the microcosm of the lower kingdoms in nature. This is the goal of all human service.

What I have said up to this point anent the Science of Impression, if read also in connection with the teaching on the Points of Revelation,* will convey much enlightenment. However, deep reflection is called for. The Science of Impression might be regarded, in the last analysis, as the fundamental science of consciousness itself, for the result of contact and impact leads to the awakening and the unfoldment of consciousness and of that growing awareness which distinguishes every form throughout the manifested

---

* *Discipleship in the New Age,* Volume II, Section 3.

world. Every form has its own area of awareness, and evolution is the process whereby forms respond to contact, react to impact, and pass on to greater development, usefulness and effectiveness. The Law of Evolution and the Science of Impression cover the unfoldment of consciousness and bring about adaptability to the immanent soul. Modern science, through its work in the fields of psychology and medicine (to mention only two) and its experiments with forms which have established the modes of constructing and bringing into being the varying mechanisms of contact found in the different kingdoms of nature, has mastered much of the evolutionary development of the exoteric response apparatus. With all this we shall not attempt to deal; it is correct as far as it goes. We shall confine ourselves to a consideration of the contacts and impacts which confront the disciples and initiates of the world today, as they work in the Hierarchy and through an Ashram, and whose path of advance is as a shining light which shineth ever more until full enlightenment has been achieved.

I would like to refer you back to page 52 where I outlined this extra-ordinary science which is—inherently in itself—the evidence of evolution, of the essential dualism in manifestation, and the testimony, unalterable and incontrovertible, to the unfoldment of consciousness. At the same time, it proceeds upon the basic premise that the various phases of consciousness which are steadily and sequentially revealed in time and space are (from the point of view of the Eternal Now) the sumtotal of the states of consciousness of the "One in Whom we live and move and have our being." All these phases of conscious acceptance of existent phenomena and their related reactions are, to Sanat Kumara, what a day's experience and reactions or the current life experiences are to the intelligent man—only vastly more enveloping and comprehensive.

There were a number of points to which I did not refer then, but which I would like to take up now in the interests of clarity and understanding. I have called this science of rapport and of reaction, the Supreme Science of Contact. That is essentially what it is. The reaction to this contact, whether cosmic as in the case of Sanat Kumara, or planetary as in the case of the Members of the Hierarchy, is nevertheless limited and circumscribed (from the point of view of the informed aspirant), is responsible for the creation of Karma or the setting in motion of causes which must unalterably have their effects—these effects being negated and rendered useless (or innocuous, if you prefer that word) when the entity concerned brings to the engendered circumstances the needed intelligence, wisdom, intuition or will. Ponder on this. Consciousness is inherent in all forms of life. That is an occult platitude. It is an innate potency which forever accompanies life in manifestation. These two, related through manifestation, are in reality atma-buddhi, spirit-reason, dedicated for the term of the creative period to a simultaneous functioning; the first result of their relation is the appearance of that which will enable the Lord of the World to express His Own unknown inscrutable purpose.

During the cycle of manifestation, this combination of life-awareness, spirit-reason, atma-buddhi, is the product of the multiplicity in unity of which we hear so much—demonstrating as activity, quality, ideology, rationality, relationship, unity, and many other expressions of the divine nature. In the earlier part of *A Treatise on the Seven Rays,* I spoke of *life, quality* and *appearance,* mentioning the major triplicity which could be and is already proven and apparent to man. Quality was emphasised as the second aspect, not because on all planes and for all time that is so, but because at the present point in human evolution, quality plus activity *appear* to be the two lower aspects of divine manifestation. Already, however, two others are, if anything, superseding them in the consciousness of thinking humanity—relationship and ideas. Still others will be rapidly added as the consciousness of man is more effectively employed.

The Science of Contact will not only reveal quality, but is revealing the lines of relationship which underlie all manifestation and of which the etheric body is the symbol. It is also rendering man sensitive to ideas as the unfolding intellect of man permits it. The reaction of humanity to these two revelations (which come, if you could but realise it, as the result, the reward, of contact and of the impact of life-reason upon that manifestation which has always been present though unrealised) will bring about vast changes and more far-reaching results than has the reaction to quality. Curiously enough, the discovery of quality as the second aspect in manifestation (later to be superseded), called for, and developed, the critical faculty in man; this critical faculty (so destructive in its present use) will be correctly expressed when the nature of relationship is better grasped and the true function of ideas is properly understood.

This Supreme Science of Contact governs all reactions to impact. This statement includes the cosmic reactions of Sanat Kumara down to the scarcely discernible reactions (invisible almost even to the eye of the seer) of the infinitesimal atom. For the sake of clarity, I divided this science into three major divisions, basing them upon the reactions of the three major planetary centres to their environment. This is a point which I would have you carefully bear in mind. I could write a treatise longer than this one purely on the creation of the response apparatus which each of these three centres of divine life-reason had to form in order to make the needed contact and to interpret correctly. There are many paradoxes in what I am here giving you, and apparently some contradictions where orthodox occultism is concerned, but that is ever the case as the teaching expands in content and the earlier all-inclusive facts are seen to be minor aspects of still greater facts. You can see, therefore, the significance and the importance of the dictum in *The Secret Doctrine* that the Hierarchy and all in the Council Chamber of Sanat Kumara (or Shamballa) have invariably passed through the human stage of evolution, for only human beings can perfectly blend and express life-reason, and only human intellect can consciously create what is needed in order to bring the needed stages of manifested life into being.

Here again emerges another reason for the importance of the "centre which we call the race of men"; upon the shoulders of humanity rests unbelievable responsibility. Therefore, whether we are dealing with simple telepathy, or with invocation and evocation, or with impression, we are in reality considering the effect of life-reason as it manifests in relation to the available and suitable environment. Note this phrase. All this takes place through men in process of being made perfect, through men who have attained a relative perfection, and through men who—in the majority of cases—arrived at perfection elsewhere than in this present manifesting cycle. This should indicate to you the potentiality hidden in the very lowest of the human family, and the future of wonder and of usefulness which lies ahead for each and all in due time and after due effort.

Technically speaking, it is the Hierarchy which is "impressed" from Shamballa, and Humanity which is reached by the Hierarchy via the method of invocation and evocation. Within the human family two things occur as the result of this received and recognised activity of a phase of the Science of Contact.

1. Telepathic relationship is set up. This, my brother, has ever existed between members of the human family and, as previously explained, is of two kinds: Solar plexus telepathy, instinctual, uncontrolled, widely prevalent and allied to many of the surprising activities of forms of life other than the human, i. e., the instinct of the homing pigeon or the method whereby cats and dogs and horses will find their homes over immense distances. The telepathic interplay between a mother and her children is instinctual and seated in the animal nature. Mental telepathy is now being recognised and studied. This is the activity and rapport established from mind to mind; it also includes the telepathic response to current

thoughtforms and thought conditions in the world today. Interest in this is already very great.

2. Intuitional telepathy begins to manifest increasingly among advanced human beings in all lands and all races. This indicates soul contact and the consequent awakening of group consciousness, for sensitivity to intuitional impressions has to do *only* with group concerns.

This Science of Contact governs relations within our *entire* planetary life and includes, for instance, the rapport being established between humanity and the domesticated animals. These animals are to their own kingdom what the New Group of World Servers is to humanity. The New Group of World Servers is the linking bridge and the mode of communication between the Hierarchy (the fifth kingdom) and Humanity (the fourth kingdom) under *the present* divine Plan; the domesticated animals fulfill, therefore, an analogous function between Humanity (the fourth kingdom) and the animal kingdom (the third). These analogies are often fertile fields of illumination.

As regards Shamballa, the impression there received is *not* the result of invocation which in due course evokes extra-planetary response, as is the case between the Hierarchy and Shamballa, and the Hierarchy and Humanity, with certain changes during the process of stepping down or of descent. That which impresses Shamballa and is received by the Grand Council of the Lord of the World, comes via Sanat Kumara because HE is in close contact with other planetary Logoi or groups of planetary Logoi, wielding a united, focussed, intelligent Will. It is Sanat Kumara Whose task it is to impress the Lives Who meet periodically in the Council Chamber with the next phase of unfolding Purpose. This Purpose is later "occultly reduced" or stepped down until it emerges as the hierarchical Plan. This Plan is contingent upon imminence, atmic realisation and pure reason, as the Hierarchy has termed these three "aspects of reaction" to impression from Shamballa. Let me make myself clear. The Hierarchy is no group of mystical workers; only those aspects of divine Purpose which can be immediately grasped and developed and which are patently valuable to humanity—when presented in right form by the Hierarchy—are registered by Them. They know what consciously to "repudiate" as it is occultly called, and They act ever in response to a Law of Imminence or of occult prevision which is almost unrecognisable and indefinable by advanced humanity. The words, "atmic realisation" are most interesting, for they refer to the quality and *the mass* of will energy which could be made available by the pledged and unified Hierarchy to carry out the imminent Plan. Never forget that in considering Shamballa and the Plan, we are thinking entirely within the limits of the expression of the WILL aspect of the Lord of the World, and this— except for advanced initiates—is well-nigh impossible. This factor has to be accepted theoretically, even if not yet understood.

To these two unalterable requirements the Hierarchy contributes the faculty of pure reason, which is the governing faculty of the Hierarchy and which brings into activity the quality to which man has erroneously given the name of "love". This emphasises the sentimental aspect and signifies to the majority, very largely, simply the sentimental and emotional aspect, which is entirely of an astral nature. Pure reason, which is the supreme characteristic of the Members of the Hierarchy, will ever express itself in right action and right human relations, and that will manifest—when present—what love in reality is. Pure love is a quality or effect of pure reason.

The pure reason of the hierarchical response is needed for the grasping and the comprehension of the Purpose as it works out through the Plan sponsored at any one time by the Hierarchy, and the quality of pure love is needed and demanded (even if unrealised) by a waiting humanity.

This "impression" emanating from Shamballa takes the form of a focussed emanation which employs the higher aspect of the antahkarana as its channel of contact. I refer not here to the thread as built by the disciple between the mental unit and the abstract mind. I refer to its continuation through the buddhic and atmic levels of consciousness into the area of magnetised consciousness (I use this word as we have not yet the necessary word to express the exact nature of this higher awareness, and the term "identification" seems somewhat unsuitable) which surrounds and protects the true Shamballa centre. It is essential that you here bear in mind that just as the mass of men do not know, recognise or respond to the Hierarchy, so—within the Hierarchy itself—you have a group analogous to this mass of men. There are many lesser members of the Hierarchy and many, very many, disciples who do not know, recognise or as yet respond to the influence or the potency of Shamballa.

Within the Hierarchy, the Science of Impression conditions the relation between senior and junior members in the various Ashrams. All do not respond in the same way, for in its higher aspects it is a science in process of mastering. It might be said, in order that you may understand more easily, that "impression" governs and conditions all those within the Hierarchy whose abstract mind is highly developed. It is not fully developed in the case of many disciples in the Ashram, and hence only certain Members of the Hierarchy (the Masters, the Adepts and Initiates of the third degree) are permitted to know the details of the Plan; these are protected by means of this very Science of Impression. The remaining members of the Hierarchy take their orders from their seniors.

I would ask you to remember that, in our planetary development, the emphasis of the entire evolutionary process is on the MIND and on the various aspects of the mind—intelligence, mental perception, the Son of Mind, the lower mind, the abstract mind, the mind as will, the Universal Mind. The three which are of major importance and which form an esoteric triangle requiring to be brought into a vital inter-relation are the Son of Mind, the abstract mind, and the Universal Mind. They are, when fully related and active, the factors which engineer divine purpose and step it down into such form that we call it the hierarchical Plan and can act upon it. Only when the initiate has attained, through monadic contact, a touch of the Universal Mind can the Purpose be sensed by him; this involves also the development of the abstract mind, plus the residue of mental perception which the Son of Mind (the soul) has bequeathed to him; through all this unfoldment he can join the group who are the Formulators of the Plan. We are dealing here with most difficult and complex matters, inherent in the initiate consciousness and for which we have as yet no correct terminology. Also, the average aspirant has no idea what is the nature of the awareness or the reactions to contact of Those Who have passed beyond the third initiation; these limitations of the average student must constantly be borne in mind.

The Science of Invocation and Evocation—which embodies the technique of interplay within the Hierarchy itself, to a certain degree between Shamballa and the Hierarchy, and to an increasing extent between Humanity and the Hierarchy—is *based entirely on a sense of relation*. Therefore only a certain level of conscious Lives can invoke Shamballa and evoke response, and this because They have Themselves developed some of the aspects of that type of mental understanding which is the hierarchical expression of the Universal Mind. The light and futile talk of certain writers and thinkers anent the cosmic ·conscious-ness, and their flippant use of such phrases as "tuning in with the Infinite" or "tapping the Universal Mind" serve only to show how very little is known in reality about the re-sponses and the reactions of those of high initiate rank or of those on the highest levels of hierarchical life.

True capacity to invoke and evoke (within initiate ranks) is based upon a mysterious development—impossible before the time of the third initiation—of the esoteric sense. The active use of the esoteric sense in the occult training offered to aspirants, disciples and initiates of lesser degree produces certain changes within the brain, with corresponding changes within the buddhic vehicle; these changes enable one at will (after the third Initiation of Transfiguration) to contact the Being, Life, or the monadic POINT of contact with Whom he will be increasingly affiliated, or the Member of the Hierarchy Whom he may desire to consult. It does not involve the use of speech or words but is simply a technical method whereby an initiate within the Hierarchy or en rapport with Shamballa can make his presence felt and certain *ideas* can be presented by him. Upon this I will not further enlarge.

For average humanity, the development of the intuition is the lower correspondence to this type of esoteric sense employed by initiates of high degree—or this mode of per-ceptive intercourse, as it is sometimes called. Within the Ashrams, advanced disciples are taught how to discover within themselves and to use this new potency and thus develop the needed mechanism. They can know simultane-ously both the demand and the answer or response which their invocation application has evoked. All disciples who have taken the third initiation have the power to invoke and to be evoked, and hence this technique is not permitted to those of lower status. A highly developed discriminative faculty is here needed. It is in reality an advanced part of the technique whereby—in the earliest stages—the disciple is permitted to attract the attention of the Master. This he does through the very importunity of his desire; later, through the use of his acquired knowledge, he proceeds to what is called "the regulated nature of his appeal." The appeal is then less regulated by desire and more under the control of will.

I am not here dealing with invocation and evocation as it is carried on between Humanity and the Hierarchy. I gave much along this line when I made public the various Invocations whereby I have been attempting to substitute the invocative method for the selfish use of prayer and the limiting mode of the average meditation process. It is a slow process by means of which this method of intercourse must be learnt and mastered, and no textbook or information on the subject is of much use. Nor am I going to deal with the ordinary telepathy prevalent among men and natural to so many, as this has been dealt with earlier in this book. But at this point I should like to emphasise something which applies to every human being. When animal-man passed through the door of individualisation and became a human being he came possessed of an innate potency of *sight;* for aeons he has seen in the three worlds, and many have for several lives sought after *the vision* which stabilises the aspirant upon the Path. Through the door of initiation, having attained the mystical vision, each aspirant will become aware of that within himself which permits of a *spiritual perception* of such an expansive nature that he gets his first real and individual glimpse of the divine Plan; from that moment his entire life is altered. Later (and this

I cannot expect the student to understand; if he thinks he does, he is being misled by words), he will pass through the door of *identification*. This is a perfectly meaningless phrase, since its significance is most carefully guarded. Symbolically speaking and in order to preserve the concept of this door in the mind of humanity, true esoteric meetings are entered on the password. Only the WORD can enter through this door—this highest and widest of all doors. Once through that door and once eligible to the Council Chamber of the Great Lord, the Initiate will comprehend what is meant by "monadic impression." It is *not* impression by *a* Monad (that meaningless term) upon the brain of a man who has constructed the antahkarana and passed the fourth initiation. It is an innate responsiveness to the Purpose of the Universal Mind of the One in Whom we live and move and have our being.

I am not indicating in any way how an individual can become telepathic. All those developments within the area or region of progressive contacts are only useful and truly available when they are developed normally and naturally and are not the result of premature unfoldment. When the development is premature there is always the danger of wrong, erroneous and self-centered interpretations. The telepathic information can be of purely selfish or personal import and that type of telepathy has no place in what I am seeking to impart. People today frequently evidence a telepathic tendency or capacity. They tune in (a phrase they regard as more euphonious than the words "telepathic rapport") with something or someone, though they know not what it is. Everything that they purport to register is regarded by them as of major importance: it is usually self-related and not due to their high point of spiritual unfoldment which warrants their being the custodians of mysterious spiritual messages—usually of a most unimportant and platitudinous nature. There are many sources of these messages and it might be useful if I here mentioned some of them; what I have to say may prove to be of value to the general occult public.

1. Messages emanating from the relatively nice, well-trained subconscious nature of the recipient. These well up from the subconscious but are regarded by the recipient as coming from an outside source. Introspective people frequently penetrate into the layer of subconscious recollection and are quite unaware of so doing. Their interest in themselves is so intense. Not knowing that they have done this,

they regard what they find as unusual, beautiful and important, and then proceed to formulate it into messages, which they expect their friends and the general public to regard as spiritually based. These messages are normally innocuous, sometimes beautiful, because they are a mixture of what the recipients have read and gathered from the mystical writing or have heard from Christian sources and the Bible. It is really the content of their right thinking along spiritual lines and can do no one any harm, but is of no true importance whatsoever. It accounts, however, for eighty-five percent (85%) of the so-called telepathic or inspired writings so prevalent at this time.

2. Impressions from the soul, which are translated into concepts and written down by the personality; the recipient is deeply impressed by the relatively high vibration which accompanies them, forgetting that the vibration of the soul is that of a Master, for the soul is a Master on its own plane. These are true soul impressions but usually have in them nothing new or of major importance; they are, again, the result of past ages of soul development (as far as the personality is concerned); they are, therefore, that which an awakening personality has contributed to the soul of the good, the true and the beautiful, plus that which has entered into the personality consciousness as a result of soul contact. This accounts for eight percent (8%) of the writings and communications put before the general public by aspirants today.

3. Teachings given by a senior or more advanced disciple on the inner planes to a disciple under training or who has just been admitted into an Ashram. These teachings bear the impress and conclusions of the senior disciple and are frequently of value; they may—and often do—contain information of which the recipient is totally unaware. The criterion here is that nothing (literally nothing) will con-

cern the recipient, either spiritually or mentally or in any other way connected with his personality, nor will they contain the platitudes of the religious background of the recipient. They will account for five percent (5%) of the teaching given, but this is in relation to the entire world and the percentage does not refer to some one occult group, one religious faith or one nation. The recognition of this is of vital importance.

4. Communications from a Master to His disciple. This accounts for two percent (2%) of the entire telepathic receptivity, demonstrated by humanity as a whole throughout the entire world. Western students would here do well to remember that the subjective Eastern student is far more prone to telepathic receptivity than is his Western brother; this has a definite bearing on all the above classifications, which is somewhat humiliating for the Western mystic and occult student. The World Scriptures emanate from another department of the second ray teaching faculty. In this statement I do not include *The Old Testament* except such passages as the Twenty-third Psalm and certain passages out of the Prophets, particularly the Prophet Isaiah. The World Scriptures were written for mystics, occupied with beauty, comfort, and encouragement, and were not written for occultists. I would call this to your attention.

In this section of the teaching I am dealing with the nature and results of contact, of receptivity. I am giving no rules for individual development, and would not, if I could. Humanity today is developing receivers of every kind of concept, beginning with the lowest of them all—the masses of men who, through demagogues, the newspapers, the radio, books and lectures, are conditioned by many minds, according to their ray type of receptivity. As true intelligence develops and as love begins to permeate human thinking, these conditioning factors will get increasingly less attractive. This means when the soul becomes of greater life importance and man-made ideas (if such a phrase is permissible) of less importance. There are, in reality, no man-made ideas. There are only ideas as grasped by the intelligentsia and then as "stepped down" by humanity's constant reaction to glamour, to emotional or astral conclusions, and to selfish interpretations.

It must be remembered that the activity of all these "impressing agencies" is felt in a wide and general sense throughout the entire planet and the planetary aura. No kingdom in nature escapes this impact, and it is thus that the purpose of the Lord of the World is carried out. Being, Coherence and Activity are thus blended into one created and creative whole; life, quality and appearance respond unitedly to the imposed intention of the planetary Logos and yet, at the same time, remain creatively free as regards their reaction to these contacted impressions; this reaction is necessarily dependent upon the type and quality of the mechanism which registers the impression. This mechanism has been developed by the life within the form throughout the creative period and—as far as the time element has been involved—the indwelling entity in any kingdom in nature has been free, and the time has been long or short, and the reaction to impression has been rapid or slow, according to the will of the controlling life. In the mineral kingdom, this reaction is very slow, for inertia or tamas controls the spiritual life within the mineral form; in the vegetable kingdom, it is more rapid, and under the invocative appeal of the lives in that kingdom the deva world is invoked and greatly aids and hastens the unfoldment of the vegetable consciousness; this is one reason for its relative sinlessness and extra-ordinary purity.

The major impression registered in the second kingdom of nature emanates from the angel worlds and from the deva hierarchy. The angels and devas are to the vegetable kingdom what the spiritual Hierarchy is to humanity. This is, of course, a mystery with which you have no concern. But impressions and reactions are to be found in both these kingdoms, and upon such response depends the evolution of the indwelling consciousness.

The animal kingdom has a peculiar relation to the fourth kingdom in nature, and the unfolding of the animal consciousness proceeds along lines paralleling, yet dissimilar to that of the human being who is beginning to respond to the kingdom of souls, the fifth kingdom. It is the karma and destiny of the fourth kingdom to be the impressing agent for the third; the problem is complicated, however, by the fact that the animal kingdom antedates the human and had, therefore, generated a measure of karma—both good and evil—prior to the appearance of mankind. The "impressing process" carried forward by humanity is modified and often negated by two factors:

1. Human ignorance and selfishness, plus inability to work consciously and intelligently with the embryonic minds within animal forms; this is true except in a few (a very few) cases which involve the domestic animals. When humanity is itself further advanced, its intelligent impression upon the consciousness of the animal kingdom will produce planetary results. At present this is not so. It will only come when the animal kingdom (as a result of human understanding) becomes invocative.

2. The self-generated karma of the animal kingdom which is largely being worked off in its relation to mankind today. The karmic entity—holding a type of rule within the third kingdom—is a part of the planetary Dweller on the Threshold.

You will note, therefore, the amazing planetary sequence of impression—all of it emanating from the highest possible sources, though stepped down and regulated to the receiving factors; all of it concerned to a greater or less degree (according to the quality of the mechanism of reception) with the will and purpose of Sanat Kumara; all of it, during the aeons, achieving a group potency and a responding sensitivity.

The main factor preventing a completely unimpeded sequence of impression from Shamballa straight down into the mineral kingdom, via all the other kingdoms, is the factor of freewill, resulting in karmic responsibility. This can be either good or bad. It is interesting to note here that both the good and the bad karma produce conditions which not only have to be worked out, but that they lead to conditions which delay what we—from our limited point of view—might look upon as the liberation of the planet. The generating of good karma necessitates the "living through" of conditions where everything (for the man responsible or for any other form within its limitations) is good, happy, beneficent and useful. The evil karma generated in any kingdom in relation to the "realm where dwelleth the planetary Dweller on the Threshold" stands between the cosmic Door of Initiation and our planetary Logos. This Dweller represents all the mistakes and errors due to wrong reactions, unrecognised contacts, deliberate choices made in defiance of known good, and mass movements and mass activities which are temporarily not progressive in time and space. I realise that where these facts apply to the subhuman kingdoms in nature you are not aware of what I mean, but that does not alter the law or movements which are in no way related to human evolution. In connection with the planetary Logos I would like to add that in that great planetary struggle and His subsequent initiation, we are all implicated—from the atom of substance up to and including all the Lives which form the Council Chamber of the Lord of the World; it is this titanic effort which is made by the sumtotal of all the living processes and entities that compose the manifestation of Sanat Kumara which is responsible for the creative evolutionary processes; it is also responsible for what we call *time,* with all that that concept involves of events, opportunity, the past, the present and the future, the good and the evil.

The dynamic impression which emanates from Shamballa reaches forth in great cycles and cyclic waves; these are impulsed from extra-planetary sources, as demanded or invoked by the Lord of the World and His Associates; they emanate in response to the "acclaimed will" of Sanat Kumara in the Council Chamber.

This high spiritual and ultimate impression moves outward along the seven rays, viewing them as seven streams of spiritual energy, qualified and coloured by the Shamballic impression; this process repeats itself when hierarchical invocation is effective and successfully established.

This again is repeated between the Hierarchy and Humanity in response to human invocation; this is becoming increasingly intelligent, potent and evocative.

The problem of the human kingdom is, however, very great. Humanity is the recipient of so many impacts, so many impressions, so many telepathic and mental currents and so many qualified vibratory impressions from all the seven kingdoms in nature that aeons have elapsed in developing the adequate discriminative sensitivity and in establishing the certitude of the point in evolution from which conscious invocation must arise and upon which the evoked impression must be registered. Unconscious invocation proceeds all the time; when it becomes conscious, it becomes exceedingly powerful.

The entire human family is today an amazing receiver of impressions, owing to its myriad types of susceptible mechanisms. These impressionable instruments are capable of registering tamasic impressions, coming from the sub-human kingdoms, particularly the third and the first; they record rajasic impressions coming from mental sources of all kinds; they are also—to a much less degree—responsive to sattvic or rhythmic impressions. Their response to these high impressions and their registration of truth, light and quality, coming from the highest sources is, however, growing.

It is because of this that the human kingdom (the great middle kingdom whose function it is to mediate between the higher and the lower) is the subject of much divine impression, conveying the Purpose of Sanat Kumara. This you know. I have taught you much along this line in *A Treatise on the Seven Rays* and also in the earlier *Treatise on Cosmic Fire*. In these present instructions I am dealing with group possibilities, with groups which can be trained to record, register and be impressed by the Hierarchy. Such a group can be in the position of being able to invoke the Hierarchy *with power* if it so choose. I am again bringing these things to your attention as aspirants and disciples, but from an angle different to those in my earlier writings. The responsibility of impressionability, of telepathic registration and of invocative appeal is very great; hence what I have written here.

XII. RELATION OF THE HUMAN TO THE
HIERARCHICAL CENTRE

True telepathic rapport is part of the Supreme Science of Contact and has peculiar and definite reference to humanity. Many different terms might be used in the effort to convey some understanding of this subtle, subjective mode of relationship, and I have used among others the following:

1. The Science of Contact.
2. The Science of Impression.
3. The Science of Invocation and Evocation.
4. The Science of Relationship.
5. The Science of Sensitivity.

All these terms convey different aspects of the reaction of form or forms to contact, to impression, to impact, to environment, to the thought context of various minds, to ascending and descending energies, to the invocation of agents and the evocation of their response. The whole planetary system is in reality a vast interlocking, interdependent and inter-related complexity of vehicles communicating or responsive to communication.

The moment that this inter-related and communicating system is studied from the angle of relationships, then the processes of evolution and the goal of the spirit of man (which is in reality the Spirit of the planetary Logos) become of vital and supreme importance, but are at the same time most difficult to comprehend. So immense is the theme that it is profitless for us to do more than deal with two factors:

1. The Science of Impression in relation to mankind.
2. The impressing Centres, as they affect the understanding of relationship.

The many modes of contact between the many subhuman and superhuman forms, groupings, and kingdoms are too intricate in their nature to be grasped at this time by students, and—which is more important—the information would be of small use to them. We will, therefore, confine ourselves to the Science of Impression and the Science of Invocation and Evocation only in so far as they affect humanity. These—from the human angle—cover *reception* of impression and of ideas, and expressions of the consequences of sensitivity at this time and in this particular cycle.

We are to consider, therefore, the relation of the human centre to the hierarchical centre and the growing responsiveness of humanity to the "Centre where the Will of God is known". As I said before, it is not my intention to give here the rules governing telepathic intercourse. Such intercourse is found between man and man and groups and groups. The relationship is slowly and normally developed and requires no hastening. It is developing as the other senses of man and his apparatus of perception have developed. Humanity is, however, outstripping telepathic development in the rapid responsiveness of entire groups, and of human beings en masse, to group impression and to group impartation of ideas. The sudden response of groups and nations to mass ideologies has been both unexpected and difficult to handle wisely and constructively. It was not anticipated by either Shamballa or the Hierarchy that mass impression would develop more quickly than that of individual sensitivity, but it has happened that way. The individual within a group and working within a group is far more correctly sensitive than is the man struggling alone to render himself sensitive to impression.

One of the factors militating against personal telepathic development lies in the fact that the strong, potent and modern ascension of the spirit in man—as a whole—frequently offsets personality reactions, and telepathy is a personality matter depending upon contact between mind and mind. The moment, however, that man *tries* to be telepathic, he is immediately swept into a vortex of abstract energies which condition him for spiritual impression far more than they fit him for personal relationships telepathically established.

This surprising development freed the supervising Masters for some of Their plans and led Them to abandon the training of individual disciples in telepathic rapport and to recognise the opportunity to train and develop invocative groups. Instead of working in lower mental substance with picked aspirants, They changed the medium of contact to that of the soul and launched the relatively new *Science of Invocation and Evocation.* The lower mind then became simply an interpreter of impressions with the emphasis upon the group mind, the group purpose and the group will. This developing system of trained invocatives made the mind a positive acting factor and tuned out all tendency to negativity.

This hierarchical decision then necessarily led to the instituting of the processes of group initiation, thus shifting the area of training and the whole of the teaching process and of preparation for initiation on to higher levels. The experiment of giving mankind the Great Invocation was tried and is proving successful, though much yet remains to be done.

It might be said, therefore, that the four requirements which are needed to aid the disciple to meet the demands of the initiatory process are "the ability to be impressed, the capacity accurately to register the impression, the power to record what has been given, and then to give it word forms in the mind consciousness." On the basis of the information received, the disciple must then properly invoke the needed energies and learn through experience to produce a responsive evocation. My earlier statement on this subject a few pages back was intended to lead up to this teaching and I repeat it here:

> "The entire human family is today an amazing receiver of impressions, owing to the myriad types of susceptible mechanisms. . . . It is because of this that the human kingdom (the great middle kingdom whose function it is to mediate between the higher and the lower) is the subject of so much divine impression, conveying the purpose of Sanat Kumara. . . . In these present instructions I am dealing with group possibilities, with groups which can be trained to record, register and be impressed by the Hierarchy. Such a group can be in the position of being able to invoke the Hierarchy *with power* if it so choose. I am again bringing these things to your attention as aspirants and disciples, but from an angle different to those in my earlier writings. *The responsibility of impressionability, of telepathic registration and of invocative appeal is very great.*"

For the aspirant and particularly for the conscious disciple, the impression to be considered comes from four sources:

1. From the disciple's own soul.
2. From the Ashram with which he is to be affiliated.
3. Directly from the Master.
4. From the Spiritual Triad, via the antahkarana.

The first two stages cover the period of the first two initiations; the third precedes the third initiation and persists until the disciple is himself a Master; the fourth type of informative impression can be registered after the third initiation and reach the disciple *in the Ashram;* he then has the task himself of impressing his mind with what he has been told and known within the Ashram; eventually, as a Master of an Ashram, he starts upon one of the major hierarchical tasks of mastering the Science of Impression. There are therefore, two aspects to this work of impression: one deals with the capacity to be impressed; the other with the ability to be an impressing agent. The disciple is not permitted to practice the art of impressing until he himself is among those who receive Triadal impression and therefore impression from Shamballa, within the protective area or aura of the Ashram with which he is affiliated. It must be remembered that this Science of Impression is in reality the science of thoughtform-making, thoughtform vitalisation and thoughtform direction; and only a disciple who has passed through the processes of Transfiguration and is no longer the victim of his own personality can be entrusted with so dangerous a cycle of powers. As long as there exists any desire for selfish power, for unspiritual control and for influence over the minds of other human beings or over groups, the disciple cannot be trusted, under the hierarchical rules, with the deliberate creation of thoughtforms designed to produce specific effects, and with their dispersal to men and groups. After he has passed the tests of the Transfiguration Initiation he may do so.

The Science of Impression is the bedrock or the foundation for the practice of telepathy. If a major world test were to be made, those receptive to impression would be found to fall into two groups:

1. Those possessing unconscious receptivity to telepathic impression. They at present constitute a majority wherein the impression is received via the solar plexus, and the thoughtforms thus generated are dispatched from the throat centre of the one who is the impressing agent.

2. Those who are developing or have developed a conscious receptivity wherein the impression is, first of all, received by the mind and then imparted to and registered by the brain. The one who is the impressing agent in this case works via the centre between the eyebrows, the ajna centre.

The first group of recipients are purely personality grounded or focussed. In some cases they are only physically aware of the life processes and of some contact which remains for them unrecognised and unchecked or uncontrolled in any way. Under this group we must, therefore, class all mediumistic phenomena, even those of the highest astral or spiritual nature, plus the messages received from the usually beautiful subconscious of the average person upon the Probationary Path. Messages from the disciple's own soul are intermediate between those mediumistic expressions and those which are definitely mental in nature.

With this last mentioned type of communication, there will be found mixed certain messages or impressions from the Ashram which the disciple will be apt to confuse with group telepathy, soul communication and direct relation with the Master—a relationship at this stage non-existent. This will not greatly matter, because when the disciple begins to realise certain differences, a new type of registration will awaken and guide the disciple's consciousness.

This stage, which embraces the second type of impression in its earliest forms, can be quite a long one, for it covers a very definite period of transition from the astral plane to the mental plane. The *time equation* varies according to ray and the age of the soul. Sixth ray people, for instance, are very slow in making this transition, owing to the pronounced factor of glamour; first and second ray people are relatively quick. Third ray people are also slow, for they are lost in the threads of their own glamorous manipulations and their devious thinking, and hardly know where truth begins and delusion ends; illusion, which is the problem of the mental types on all rays, is far more temporary in its effects than is delusion.

When the disciple has mastered to some degree the significant difference between messages from his own subconscious or the subconscious of other people with whom he may be en rapport, and the messages coming from his own soul, his life then becomes more self-directed and organised, more fruitful from the angle of service, and therefore of definite use to the Hierarchy. He learns to distinguish the messages coming from his own soul from those which are hierarchical; his life becomes more clearly directed; he next distinguishes definitely and accurately the communications which come to him from the Ashram and which are sent out to make impression upon the minds of aspirants and disciples of all degrees and of all ray types. When he can distinguish between these various communications, then and only then does the third type of communication become possible—direct messages which are due to contact with the Master of his Ashram in person. He, by that time, possesses what has been called "the freedom of the Ashram" and "the keys to the Kingdom of God"; he can then be trusted with some of the directive potency of the Ashram itself. His thinking will then affect and reach others. This developing effectiveness grows with rapidity when the fourth type of impression is familiar to the disciple: that coming from the Spiritual Triad, and therefore from the Monad and Shamballa. There are consequently (to this final stage of impression) three lesser though definite states, each marking an expansion in the realm of service and each related to the last three initiations of the total possible nine initiations which confront developing humanity. The sixth initiation, in which only Masters can participate, marks a transition from the first three stages of impressibility required by the disciples as preludes to the fifth initiation—or in reality to the third, fourth and fifth—and are related to the three stages of Triadal communication, each of which is related to the seventh, the eighth and the ninth initiations.

Never does the geometrical pattern, the numerical progression or the Law of Correspondences break down in the understanding of the purpose and the plans of the planetary Logos—established before the worlds were created and finding their prototypes upon the *cosmic* mental planes. These points are peculiarly difficult for men to grasp at this time wherein their state of consciousness is concentratedly individualised.

Nevertheless, there is on man's part a steadily growing responsiveness to an expanding environment, as for instance man's recognition of the distinction between nationalism and inter-nationalism. This responsiveness is naturally conditioned by human freewill, *effective peculiarly in the timing process*. He may learn rapidly and fast or he may go the slow way, but his state of consciousness remains one of a developing reaction to his environment, as registered by his consciousness, and in which he (stage by stage) becomes an integral factor. This integration into his environment, his absorption of its atmosphere and his potency in progression are all related to the fact that he is created to receive impression and that he possesses a mechanism of response to all the facets of the divine expression in manifestation. It is for that reason that the truly illumined man and all who have taken the three highest initiations are always referred to as "the diamond souled"; they, in their totality constitute the "jewel in the lotus"—that twelve-petalled lotus which is the symbol and expression of the potency of the planetary Logos.

You can see, therefore, how the theme of revelation runs throughout the entire evolutionary process; it must never be forgotten that step by step, stage by stage, expansion after expansion, initiation after initiation, the divine WHOLE is realised by man. The method is impressed from a hitherto unrecognised environment; this only becomes possible in this particular form when "the Sons of Mind who are the Sons of God and whose nature is at-one with His began to move on Earth". The Science of Impression is in reality the technique whereby Humanity has been taught by the Spiritual Hierarchy from the moment of its first appearance upon Earth; it is the technique which all disciples have to learn (no matter which of the Seven Paths they may eventually choose) and it is also the sublime art which every Master practices on inspiration from Shamballa; it is a technique which is implemented by the Will, and its consummation is the complete assimilation of the "little wills of men" into the divine Purpose; it is the acceptance on their part of the promotion of that Purpose through right impression on all forms of life at any particular point of evolution. Disciples then become agents of the divine will and are entrusted with the direction of energies, with the plan and with the secrets and the inspiration which are hidden in the Mind of God.

To that knowledge—germinated and formed in the solar system previous to this—they add that which the present solar system has to give and to mature; the magnetic attractiveness of the second Ray of Love-Wisdom in one of its three major forms or Rays of Aspect, implemented by the four Rays of Attribute. This power to use the ray energies to attract and impress the constantly expanding revelation is the clue to all the work going forward today, and to this activity we give the name of the Science of Impression. It involves the constant opening up of a new environment—an environment which reaches all the way from the lowest grade of daily living, undertaken by the least developed of human beings, to that point upon the ladder of evolution when the aspirant becomes consciously susceptible to what we call spiritual impression. At that point he becomes capable of being more sensitive to a higher range of impression and—at the same time—he himself begins to learn the art of impressing the minds of others, to master the understanding of the level from which he works as an impressing agent, and to know who are the sons of men he can impress. He has to master also the secondary lesson of adapting his environment in such a manner that he can impress others and the impression can find its way through his environing circumstances and into the usually inattentive minds for whom he feels a responsibility.

This he does through a growing knowledge of himself and through learning the *art of registering*. The clearer and the more deeply apprehending is his capacity to register the impression to which he is subjected and to which he is sensitive, the more easily will he reach those he must aid towards a wider and deeper insight. This registering of his own expanding environment—with all its implications of a new vision, a new goal, a wider field of service—leads to the inflowing energies (arriving on the wings of inspiration) becoming a reservoir of thought-substance, to the use of which he must accustom himself.

The first step then is *the fact of recording* and of reducing into correct and available concepts, ideas and thoughtforms, that which he has registered. This marks the first stage in his truly occult service, and to this new type of service he will be increasingly *dedicated*. From the reservoir of thought-substance he learns to project those forms, those magnetic ideas, which will invoke the attention of those he seeks to help; this is called the stage of *resultant invocation*. It is an invocative act, an invocative way of living, which will find its way into the minds of men, and which will call forth or evoke from them a response and a widening consciousness; the processes of spiritual impression are thereby set up; it is also an invocation—on the part of the disciple—for further and greater impression and inspiration in order to increase his ability to serve.

You will have noticed that I have given no instructions as to the art of developing telepathic sensitivity. The reason is, as I told you before, that this sensitivity should be, and always is, a normal unfoldment when the disciple is correctly oriented, completely dedicated and learning decentralisation. If it is a forced process, then the sensitivity developed is not normal and carries with it much difficulty and future danger. Where the disciple is concerned, release from the constant consideration of personal circumstances and problems leads inevitably to a clear mental release; this then provides *those areas of free mental perception which make the higher sensitivity possible*. Gradually, as the disciple acquires true freedom of thought and the power to be receptive to the impression of the abstract mind, he creates for himself a reservoir of thought which becomes available at need for the helping of other people and for the necessities of his growing world service. Later, he becomes sensitive to impression from the Hierarchy. This is at first purely ashramic, but is later transformed into total hierarchical impression by the time the disciple is a Master; *the Plan is then the dynamic substance providing the content of the reservoir of thought upon which he can draw*. This is a statement of unique and unusual importance. Later still, he becomes sensitive to impression from Shamballa, and the quality of the Will which implements planetary Purpose is added to the content of his available knowledge. The point which I seek to make here, however, is the fact of the existence of a growing reservoir of thought which the disciple has created in response to the many varying impressions to which he is becoming increasingly sensitive; the ideas, concepts and spiritual objectives of which he is becoming aware are steadily being formulated by him into thoughts with their appropriated thoughtforms, and upon these he learns to draw as he seeks to serve his fellowmen. He finds himself in possession of a reservoir or pool of thought-substance which is the result of his own mental activity, of his innate receptivity, and which provides the material for teaching and the "fount of knowledge" upon which he can draw when he seeks to aid other people.

The essential point to be grasped is that sensitivity to impression is a normal and natural unfoldment, parallelling spiritual development. I gave you a clue to the entire process when I said that

> *"Sensitivity to impression involves the engendering of a magnetic aura upon which the highest impressions can play."*

I would have you give the deepest consideration to these words. As the disciple begins to demonstrate soul quality, and the second divine aspect takes possession of him and controls and colours his entire life, automatically the higher sensitivity is developed; he becomes a magnet for spiritual ideas and concepts; he attracts into his field of consciousness the outline, and later the details, of the hierarchical Plan; he becomes aware eventually of the planetary Purpose; all these impressions are not things which he must seek out and learn laboriously to ascertain, to hold and seize upon. They drop into his field of consciousness *because* he has created a magnetic aura which invokes them and brings them "into his mind". This magnetic aura begins to form itself from the first moment he makes a contact with his soul; it deepens and grows as those contacts increase in frequency and become eventually an habitual state of consciousness; then, at will and at all times, he is en rapport with his soul, the second divine aspect.

It is this aura which is in reality the reservoir of thought-substance upon which he can spiritually rely. His point of focus is upon the mental plane. He is no longer controlled by the astral nature; he is successfully constructing the antahkarana along which the higher impressions can flow; he learns not to dissipate this inflow but to accumulate within the aura (with which he has surrounded himself) the knowledge and the wisdom which he realises his service to his fellowmen requires. A disciple is a magnetic centre of light and knowledge just in so far as the magnetic aura is held by him in a state of receptivity. It is then constantly invocative of the higher range of impressions; it can be evoked and set into "distributing activity" by that which is lower and which is demanding aid. The disciple therefore, in due time, becomes a tiny or minute correspondence of the Hierarchy—invocative as it is to Shamballa and easily evoked by human demand. These are points warranting careful consideration. They involve a primary recognition of points of tension and their consequent expansion into magnetic auras or areas, capable of invocation and evocation.

These areas of sensitivity pass through three stages, upon which it is not my intention to enlarge:

1. Sensitivity to impression from other human beings. This sensitivity becomes of use in service *when* the needed magnetic aura has been engendered and is brought under scientific control.

2. Sensitivity to group impression—the passage of ideas from group to group. The disciple can become a receptive agent within any group of which he is a part, and this ability indicates progress in his part.

3. Sensitivity to hierarchical impressions, reaching the disciple via the antahkarana and—later—from the Hierarchy as a whole, when he has attained some of the higher initiations. This indicates ability to register impression from Shamballa.

It would be of value if we now considered three points which are concerned with sensitivity to impression, with the construction of the resultant reservoir of thought, and with responsiveness to subsequent invocative appeals. These three points are:

1. Processes of Registration.
2. Processes of Recording Interpretations.
3. Processes of Resultant Invocative Response.

I would recall to your minds the knowledge that the aura which each of you has created around the central nucleus of your incarnated self or soul is a fragment of the overshadowing soul which brought you into manifestation. This aura is (as you well know) composed of the emanations of the etheric body, and this in its turn embodies three types of energy for which you are individually responsible. These three types are (when added to the energy of prana which composes the etheric vehicles):

1. The health aura. This is essentially physical.
2. The astral aura, which is usually by far the most dominant factor, extensive and controlling.
3. The mental aura, which is in most cases relatively small but which develops rapidly once the disciple takes his own development *consciously* in hand, or once the polarisation of the personality is upon the mental plane. The time will eventually come when

the mental aura will obliterate (if I may use such an inadequate term) the emotional or astral aura, and then the soul quality of love will create a substitute, so that the needed sensitivity does not entirely disappear but is of a higher and far more acute nature.

In this threefold aura (or more correctly, fourfold, if you count the etheric vehicle) every individual lives and moves and has his being; it is this living, vital aura which is the recording agent of all impressions, both objective and subjective. It is this "agent of sensitive response" which the indwelling self has to control and use in order to register impression or to direct etheric or mental impression out into the world of men. Astral impression is purely selfish and individual and, though it may affect a man's surroundings, is not directed as are the other energies registered. It is the aura which predominantly creates the effects which a person has upon his associates; it is not primarily his words which produce reactions even though they are supposed to embody his reactions and his thinking but which are, in reality, usually expressions of his emotional desires.

All of us, therefore, carry around with us a subjective mechanism which is a true and perfect picture of our peculiar point in evolution. It is the aura which a Master watches, and this is a factor of major importance in the life of the disciple. The light of the soul within the aura and the condition of the various aspects of the aura indicate whether or not the disciple is nearing the Path of Discipleship. As the emotional reactions lessen, and as the mental apparatus clarifies, the progress of the aspirant can be exactly noted. I would have you distinguish carefully between the astral and the mental bodies and that which they emanate. The bodies (so called) are substantial in nature; the aura is essentially radiatory and extends from each substantial vehicle in every direction. This is a point which should be most carefully noted.

The problem of the aspirant as he "engenders" his magnetic aura is himself to withdraw, and thus lessen the extent and the power of the astral aura, and extend and increase the potency of the mental aura. It should be remembered that the large majority of aspirants are definitely polarised in the astral nature, and that therefore their problem is to achieve a different polarisation and to become focussed upon the mental plane. This takes time and vast effort. Eventually—as mentioned above—the radiation of the soul is substituted in place of the hitherto present emotional activity of the aspirant; this emanation is, in reality, a radiation from the love petals of the egoic lotus.

The moment an aspirant begins to work *consciously* at his own unfoldment and to consider and deal with the aura with which he is equipped, he then passes through three stages during his progress upon the Path of Return. These are:

1. The stage wherein he discovers the potency and the quality of his astral aura. Owing to the fact that this is (in this second solar system) the quality of love and its distortion into the astral nature, the development of emotional sensitivity is peculiarly and almost unnaturally strong. It is stronger than the mental body and its mental direction.

2. The stage wherein the mental vehicle increases its potency and produces, finally, a mental radiation which is so strong that it dominates and controls the astral aura.

3. The stage wherein the soul expresses its essential nature of love and begins to pour its radiation into the astral aura, via the astral body. Eventually the

sensitivity of love is substituted for emotional sensitivity and desire.

Aspirants are to be found at all these three stages of sensitivity. There comes a moment during the second initiation when the soul of the initiate sweeps into activity and fundamental force (if I might use such a term) submerges the astral nature, vitalising and inspiring the astral body, changing temporarily the quality of the astral aura, and establishing a control which will lead finally to the substitution which I have mentioned above. This is an aspect of the truth which underlies the doctrine of "vicarious atonement"—a doctrine which has been woefully distorted by Christian theology.

Let us now deal with the aforementioned "Processes of Registration, of Recording Interpretations, and the Resultant Invocative Response." We must bear in mind always that I am stating general rules and that I am not dealing either with the ideal or with the undesirable; the *sources of impression* change as the disciple makes progress, though always the larger and the greater source will include all lesser sources.

The fact that a man is sensitive to hierarchical impression in his mental aura will not prevent his being sensitive in his astral nature to the invocative and emotional call of human beings. The two together are most useful in effect, if the disciple sees to it that they are related. Forget this not, brother of mine. The *capacity to interpret* recorded impressions is likewise learnt as the mental aura develops under the influence of the "mind held steady in the light" of the soul; the disciple learns that all recorded truth is susceptible to many interpretations, and that these unfold with increasing clarity as he takes one initiation after another, and as he develops conscious responsiveness. The *ability to invoke* demonstrates from life to life and involves the invocation of conscious response from the anima mundi or from the subconscious soul of all things, as well as from the human consciousness and from the world of super-conscious contact.

This ability develops steadily as the aspirant treads the Path of Discipleship; it is frequently prefaced in the earlier stages by much confusion, much astral psychism and frequent wrong interpretations. There is no need at this stage, however, for undue distress, because all that is needed is experience, and that experience is gained through experiment and its expression in the daily life. In no case is the truism of learning through a system of trial and error proved more correct than it is in the life and experience of the accepting disciple. When he is an accepted disciple, the errors decrease in number even though the trials (or the experimental use of the many varying energies) become more extensive and, therefore, cover a much wider range of activities.

The *Processes of Registration* are founded upon what I might call invocative approaches from a wide area of possible contacts. The disciple has to learn to distinguish between these many impacts upon his sensitive aura. In the early stages the majority of them are unconsciously registered, though the registration is acute and accurate; the goal, nevertheless, is *conscious* registration; this is brought about through the constant and steady holding of the attitude of the Observer. It is developed through the attainment of detachment—the detachment of the Observer from all desires and longings which concern the separated self. It will therefore be obvious to you that the use of the word "observer" involves the concept of duality and, therefore, of separation. In this case, however, the motive prompting observation is not self-interest, but the determination to clarify the aura so that it can register only that which will be illuminating and related to the divine Plan, which will be to the benefit of humanity and, therefore, to the creation of a new server within the Ashrams of the Hierarchy.

The divisions made by certain psychologists of the consciousness of man into subconscious, conscious or self-conscious, and superconscious have a real measure of value here. It must be remembered, however, that the disciple, first of all, becomes a truly conscious unit of humanity and thus develops a true self-consciousness. This he arrives at by discriminating between the lower self and the higher self, and this renders his magnetic aura sensitive to an aspect of himself which has not hitherto been a controlling factor. From that achieved point he begins to register impressions with increasing clarity and accuracy. Usually, in the early stages, the one desire of the disciple is to register impressions from the Hierarchy; he much prefers that idea to the idea of registering impressions from his own soul or from the surrounding human factors, his fellowmen and the environment and the circumstances which they create. He longs for what might be called "vertical impression." This motive, being very largely self-centredness, turns the disciple introspectively in upon himself, and it is in this stage that many aspirants become prisoners, astrally speaking, because they register in their magnetic aura the many astrally motivated thoughtforms of what they believe and hope "vertical impression" supposedly would convey. They contact with facility the astral counterparts of the higher worlds, which are reflected (and thereby distorted) into the astral plane; the world there registered is glamoured by wrong and selfish desires and by the wishful thinking of well-meaning devotees. Upon this I need not enlarge. All disciples—at some point or another of their training—have to work through this phase of glamour; in so doing they clarify and intensify the magnetic aura and, simultaneously, clarify the surrounding astral world with which they are in contact. They learn also that the longing to register impressions from the Hierarchy *must* give place to the determination to place their magnetic aura at the disposal of humanity; they then learn to register human need and to understand thereby where help is possible and their fellowmen can be served. By means of this conscious registration of invocative appeals from the world of horizontal contacts, the magnetic aura of the disciple is cleared of the hindering and engrossing thoughtforms, and from the aspirational desires and longings which have hitherto prevented right registration. The disciple then ceases to create them, and those which have been created die out or atrophy for lack of attention.

Later on, when the accepting disciple becomes the accepted disciple and is permitted to participate in ashramic activity, he adds the ability to register hierarchical impression; this however is only possible *after* he has learnt to register impression coming to him from his own soul (the vertical impression) and from the surrounding world of men (the horizontal impression). When he has taken certain important initiations, his magnetic aura will be capable of registering impression from the subhuman kingdoms in nature. Again, later on, when he is a Master of the Wisdom and, therefore, a full member of the fifth kingdom in nature, the world of hierarchical life and activity will be the world from which *horizontal* impression will be made upon his magnetic aura, and *vertical* impression will come from the higher levels of the Spiritual Triad and, still later, from Shamballa. Then the world of humanity will be to him what the subhuman kingdoms were when the fourth kingdom, the human, was the field of his registered horizontal impression.

You have here the true significance of the Cross of humanity clearly revealed.

The fact of registration is no unusual phenomenon. Sensitive people are constantly being impressed from some level of consciousness or other, and are receptive to these impressions according to the level of consciousness upon which they normally function; mediums, for instance, are exceedingly prone to receive impressions from etheric or astral levels, as are the vast majority of astral psychics—and their name is legion. Impressions from mental levels (concrete, abstract or of a more exalted nature) make their impress upon the minds of those who have attained a true measure of focus upon the mental plane. Scientists, mystics, mathematicians, occult students, aspirants and disciples, educators and humanitarians and all who love their fellowmen are all susceptible to such impression, and one of the outstanding needs of the disciple is to develop adequate sensitivity to ashramic impression and contact. Then he moves out of the group of mental sensitives listed above.

The problem with which I now deal is far deeper and concerns the interpretation and the clear and correct recording of the impression, which is a far more difficult matter. The subject who is impressed must know the source of the impression; he must be able to relate it to some field of demanded information, correction, instruction, or energy distribution. He must be able to state clearly on what aspect of his recording mechanism (the mind, the astral body, the energy body, or the brain) the imparted and registered impression has made impact. One of the difficulties, for instance, facing the aspiring disciple and the earnest occult student is to record directly *in the brain* impressions from the Spiritual Triad (and later from the Monad), via the antahkarana.

This impression must be a direct descent from mental levels to the brain, avoiding all contact with the astral body; only in so far as this direct descent is attained will the recorded impression be devoid of error. It will not then be tinctured with any emotional complex whatsoever, for it is the astral level of consciousness which is the great distorter of essential truth. Impressions from the Ashram or from the Spiritual Triad (which are the only type of impressions with which I am here concerned) pass through three stages:

1. *The stage of mental recording.* The clarity and the accuracy of this recording will be dependent upon the condition of the channel of reception, the antahkarana; in this recording, curiously enough, a certain *element of time* enters in. It is not time as you know it upon the physical plane, which is but the registration by the brain of passing "events"; it is the higher mental correspondence to time. Into this, I cannot here enter as the theme is too abstruse; for time, in this connection, is related to distance, to descent, to focus, and to the power to record.

2. *The stage of brain reception.* The accuracy of this reception will be dependent upon the quality of the physical brain cells, upon the polarisation of the thinking man in the head centre, and the freedom of the brain cells from all emotional impression. The difficulty lies here, that the receiving aspirant or the focussed thinker is always aware emotionally of the descent of the higher impression and of the consequent clarification of the theme of his thought. This must, however, be recorded by a perfectly quiescent astral vehicle, and therefore you will see one of the main objectives of true meditation.

3. *The stage of recognised interpretation.* This is an exceedingly difficult phase. Interpretation is dependent upon many factors: the educational background, the point reached in evolution, the mystical or the occult approach of the disciple to the centre of truth, his freedom from the lower psychism, his essential humility (which plays a major part in proper understanding), and his personality decentralisation. In fact, the character in its entirety is involved in this important matter of correct interpretation.

In this aspect of impression the subject of SYMBOLS must necessarily be involved. All impressions must necessarily be translated and interpreted in symbols, in word forms or in pictorial representations; these the aspirant cannot avoid; and it is in the word forms (which are, needless to point out, in the nature of symbols) that he is apt to go astray. They are the media through which the registered impression is conveyed to the brain consciousness, i.e., to the physical plane awareness of the disciple, thus making possible his useful comprehension of abstract ideas or of those aspects of the Path which it is his duty to understand and teach.

There is no need for me to elaborate this theme. The true disciple is ever aware of the possibility of error, of the intervention of psychic intrusions and distortions; he knows well that true and effective interpretation of the imparted impression is dependent largely upon the purity of the receiving channel and upon the freedom of his nature from all aspects of the lower psychism—a point oft forgotten. A thick veil of concrete thoughtforms can also distort the true interpretation, as can astral intervention; the teaching upon the Path and the spiritual impression can be interfered with by glamour from the astral plane or by separative and concrete ideas emanating from mental levels. In this case it can be truly said that "the mind is the slayer of the real." There is a deep occult significance to the words "an open mind"; it is as essential to correct interpretation as is freedom from glamour and the psychic expressions to be found upon the astral plane.

Here again you can grasp the necessity of *a factual alignment* so that a direct channel is created, along which the impression (directed by some higher source than the personality) can descend into the brain. At first, this channel and alignment must be established between the brain and the soul; this will involve all the three aspects of the personality—the etheric body, the astral vehicle and the mind nature; basically, this aligning process should be started and developed upon the Probationary Path and brought to a relatively high state of effectiveness upon the earlier stages of the Path of Discipleship. Later, as the disciple consciously creates the antahkarana and becomes a functioning part of the Ashram, he learns (whilst practicing alignment) to by-pass—if I may use such a word—two aspects of himself which have hitherto been of major importance: the astral vehicle and the soul body or causal body. The astral body is thus by-passed before the fourth initiation, and the soul body before the fifth; the entire process of "by-passing" takes much time and must be worked at with intensity, first of all with the focus upon the emotional nature through conscious discrimination, and finally upon the soul nature under the inspiration of the Spiritual Triad which is eventually substituted for the soul. All this will take many incarnations. For the registration and the interpretation of the higher impressions is a basic occult science and takes much learning and application to perfect.

As the two processes are slowly developed, the third stage automatically becomes increasingly effective. The re-

ceived and interpreted impression brings about fundamental
changes in the life and the state of consciousness of the aspirant and, *above all, in his orientation. He becomes an
evocative and invocative centre of energy.* That which he
has received through the medium of his aligning channel
becomes a potent factor in invoking a fresh flood of higher
impression; it also makes him evocative upon the physical
plane, so that the magnetic aura which he has engendered
becomes increasingly sensitive to these spiritual inflowing
impressions, and also increasingly sensitive to that which he
evokes from his surrounding physical environment and from
humanity. He becomes a power station en rapport with the
Hierarchy and he receives and distributes (in response to
the evocative call of humanity and human need) the energy
received. He also becomes a "receiver of light" and of
spiritual illumination, and a distributor of light in the dark
places of the world and into human hearts. He is, therefore,
an invocative and evocative centre for use by the Hierarchy
in the three worlds of human evolution.

The word *telepathy* has been used primarily to cover the many phases of mental contact and the exchange of thought without the use of the spoken or written word or sign. However, what is thus understood in this modern usage does not cover the higher aspects of "relationship within the Universal Mind." The third aspect, that of intelligence, is involved when interpretation of contact occurs; the second aspect, that of love-wisdom, is the factor which makes the higher impression possible, and this it does whilst that aspect is developing or in process of coming into functioning activity. During this developing process, only straight telepathy is possible and this is of two kinds:

1. *Sympathetic telepathy* or immediate understanding, awareness of events, apprehensions of happenings, and identification with personality reactions. This is all connected with the solar plexus activity of the personality and this—when the love nature or second aspect is unfolded or unfolding—becomes the "seed or germ" of the intuitive faculty. The entire process is, therefore, astral-buddhic and involves the lower aspects of the Universal Mind as an agent.

2. *Mental telepathy* or the interplay of transmitted thought. Though this is a constant phenomenon among advanced intellectual people, it is still scarcely recognised, its laws and modes of expression are as yet unknown, and the best minds and interpreters on subjective levels still confuse it with solar plexus reactions. It is a relatively new and unexplored sci-

ence, but the range of its activities is *not* astral and, therefore, related to the solar plexus centre, for the substance in which this science is carried forward is not astral substance but mental substance, and therefore another vehicle is involved and employed, that of the mental body. It is the "seed or germ" of higher contacts and of impressions coming from levels higher than the buddhic or intuitional plane. It is related to the higher aspect of the Universal Mind, to the intelligent Will. In both cases, the lower aspect of love (emotional and sensitive astral response) and the pure love of the soul are involved.

Astral, sympathetic sensitivity is fallible and frequently erroneous in its conjectures and interpretations. The higher telepathy—also a form of sensitivity, and which is as an entering door or concept—becomes eventually infallible; in its earlier stages (where methods of interpretation and of deduction are concerned) it may prove frequently at fault.

Straight mental telepathy is one of the highest demonstrations of the personality; it is in the nature of a bridging faculty, for it is one of the major steps towards the higher impression; it always presupposes a relatively high stage of mental development, and that is one reason why it is not yet regarded as a reputable, proved and provable capacity of the human being. In this case, the mind is truly "the slayer of the Real," and the sources and modes of subjective knowledge still remain in a dark area of the human consciousness. The normal processes of evolution will, however, prove incontrovertibly the existence of faculties which make the higher spiritual and subjective impressions possible, and eventually normal.

This "Supreme Science of Contact" can be—as already explained—broken up into the following phases which are all progressively developed from each other. Forget not the inevitable continuity which is the outstanding characteristic of the evolutionary process.

1. *Astral sensitive awareness.* This is based upon the reactions of the solar plexus, and the entire process is carried forward upon the astral plane and with astral substance. This, in its highest form, becomes the factor which later makes intuitive awareness and intuitive sensitivity possible; then the process is carried forward in buddhic substance. Aspirants are, at one stage of their development, strongly astral-buddhic in nature. This should be remembered.

2. *Mental telepathy.* This involves naturally two minds or several minds, and the process is carried forward in the substance of the mental plane. It is the factor which makes possible the activity which we call "impression." This impression comes largely from certain aspects of the mental plane, such as:

   a. The soul of the telepathic individual, using the knowledge petals of the egoic lotus—a high form of mental intelligence.

   b. The abstract mind, so called. This aspect of mental substance is largely used by the Hierarchy in order to reach the minds of disciples. It is only within the last few centuries that the Hierarchy has shifted the focus of its living attention on to the buddhic plane and away from the mental plane. This has become possible *because* the aspirants of the world are now sensitive to contacts which are founded upon an astral-buddhic consciousness but which are strictly carried on within mental substance. This necessarily involves the three aspects of the mind, found therein: the concrete mind, the Son of Mind, and the abstract sensitivity or reaction. This involves (on the physical plane) an activity of the pituitary body (as you can readily see) and also the use of the ajna centre.

3. *The occult Science of Impression.* This becomes possible when the other two forms of telepathic rapport are present and are developing to a certain point of accuracy. It is dependent also upon the construction of the antahkarana and upon the steady orientation of the aspirant or disciple toward the Spiritual Triad; it also becomes possible when the abstract mind is developed and sensitive, and can thus become the seed or germ of the spiritual Will; this will involve responsiveness to divine purpose. The higher aspect of this abstract mind is the atmic plane. It is useful to realise the substantial nature of these two levels of consciousness. It is within the substance of the atmic plane that the activity is set up which can impress the abstract mind, which then becomes the seat of the consciousness of the spiritual man; at the same time, he remains in active possession and use of his personality and continues to employ the concrete mind; astral sensitivity, however, then begins to fall *below the threshold of consciousness* and thus joins the great array of instincts and of instinctual reactions of which the human being is possessed and which admit him into the life and conditioned awareness of all that exists in the three worlds, including the three subhuman kingdoms of nature. It is with these subliminated and

controlled instincts that those Masters and disciples work whose task it is to oversee the evolution of the forms of life in the subhuman kingdoms.

The higher forms of mental telepathy, involving the soul and the abstract mind are concerned solely with the divine Plan—as the Hierarchy works it out in the three worlds. The Science of Impression is concerned, therefore, primarily, with the divine Purpose as Shamballa is working it out, and also with those higher aspects of hierarchical work which are not concerned with work in the three worlds. This is a point upon which I would ask you to ponder.

Today, owing to the curious evolutionary stage reached in the human kingdom, an intermediate aspect of the three above forms of impression has been instituted; it is like an interim period between full human expression and the full expression of the kingdom of souls. This we call:

4. *The Science of Invocation and Evocation.* This science can and does use the unintelligent urges and the higher (yet inchoate) longings of the masses of men in an invocative form; it does so in order to bridge the gap existing in consciousness between the life of the ordinary man, the life of the integrated personality and the life of the soul. Through the use of this invocative demand—oft speechless and not consciously expressed—the disciples of the world can focus; they can employ it and thus generate an energy which will be strong enough to make a true impact and a definite impression upon Beings and Lives found on levels higher than those in the three worlds. This impact evokes a reaction from these higher Beings, and then a spiritual and intelligent interplay is set up which is of great value in pro-

moting an added stimulus and an increased vitalisation of the normal and usually slow evolutionary process. This is happening today in an acute form and accounts for much that is taking place in the world of human affairs at this time. The spreading stimulation is of a very intense nature. The invocative cry of humanity is not only the voiceless appeal which the hierarchical workers are everywhere mobilising, but it finds expression also in all the plans and schemes, the formulated platforms, and the many groups and organisations which are dedicated to the betterment of human living.

Certain basic concepts underlie every phase of the Science of Contact, and without them there would be no basis for any effort to master this science. Please grasp this fact. There are three which must always be borne in mind:

1. *The medium through which the thought currents or impressions* (from no matter what source) *must pass* in order to make an impact upon the human brain *is the planetary etheric body.* This is fundamental in its implications. This etheric vehicle makes all relationships possible, because the individual etheric body is an integral part of the vital body of the planet. This vital body is the medium also of all instinctual reactions, such as an animal will evidence when danger is around. The closer that this etheric body is interwoven (if I may use such a word) with the dense physical vehicle, the clearer will be the instinctual reaction—as in the illustration which I have given and which is based upon millenia of such reactions; the greater also will be the sensitivity and the more aptitude will there be for tele-

pathic contact and recognition of the higher impressions. It might also be added that the etheric body of a disciple or even of an advanced person can be so handled and dealt with that it can reject much that might otherwise impinge upon it, pass through it or use it as a channel. This training is automatic; evidence of it can also be seen in the ability which the human mechanism possesses to tune out all contacts and impressions that it may not need, to which it is so accustomed that they do not even register, and all that it deems undesirable or not fit for consideration. The reason that true telepathic contact between minds is not more prevalent is due to the fact that few people think with an adequate clarity or with the energy required; they do not create true, concise or powerful thoughtforms or—if they do—these thoughtforms are not correctly directed towards the intended objective. When a man is a disciple and deliberately seeks to be impressed by his soul, by the Master or by the Spiritual Triad, the task of the impressing agent is relatively simple; all the disciple has to do is to develop right receptivity, plus an intuitive intelligence which will enable him to make correct interpretations, and to recognise also the source of the communication or impression.

This brings us to the second basic concept:

2. *Sensitivity to impression involves the engendering of a magnetic aura upon which the highest impressions can play.* This I dealt with (in some measure) in the preceding section. It should be borne in mind that the potency of the magnetic aura which envelops all human beings is to be found at present in four

areas of substance; these four areas are close to four major centres. When the individual is strictly low grade and is predominantly animal in nature, then the majority of impacting impressions will reach him automatically through the sacral centre; such impacting impressions (as you can well imagine) will be heavy and yet dynamic; they will have reference to all that concerns his physical being, his physical appetites, and his physical comfort or discomfort. There are however, today, relatively few persons in proportion to the planetary population who use the sacral centre as the major registering organ. The magnetic aura (when this is the case) is relatively small; all the tendencies of this tiny aura are downward in nature, and all impressions (which cannot possibly come from a higher source than the man himself) work *down* through the aura of the sacral centre. Most of the impressions are therefore purely instinctual in nature and little or no thought is involved; there is evidence, however, of what can be understood as aspiration even if it is not what a true aspirant might regard as spiritual in nature.

The average, though still unthinking, human being works through his astral body and, because he is there polarised, works through his solar plexus centre—etherically and primarily. All impressions find entrance into the aura via the area around that part of the etheric vehicle. It is through this major centre that the ordinary medium works, receiving impressions and communications from astral entities or from the animated astral forms to be found in the glamours created by humanity.

Forget not, nevertheless, that true aspiration is essentially an astral product or reaction; all aspi-

rants—in the early stages of their slow re-orienta-
tion—work through the solar plexus centre, and thus
only gradually focus the lower energies there, prior
to their transmutation and elevation to the higher
centre, the heart centre. There are certain disciples
who work deliberately upon the astral plane, under
instruction from the Master of their Ashram, in
order to reach such neophytes and thus to impress
them with the knowledge and the subtle information
needed for their progress. No Master works in this
manner, and the Masters have therefore to use certain of Their disciples in this service. Such disciples
direct the desired impression to the solar plexus area
of the magnetic aura. This magnetic aura has another point of entry in the region of the throat centre, utilising it as the recipient of higher impressions.
This centre or area of energy is largely used and
vitally activated by those who are the creative workers of the world; they have necessarily made a direct
contact with the soul and are therefore wide open
to those intuitive ideas which are the source of their
creative work. According to the success they have
in such creative production, and according to the
beauty of their work, will be the impression they
thereby convey to other men. Curiously enough, the
new and peculiar forms of art which delight some
people and which outrage the sense of beauty in
others are largely solar plexus creations and are
therefore *not* of a truly high order. In a few of
them—a very few—the throat centre is involved.

The magnetic aura around the head is that which
is truly sensitive to the highest impressions and is
the point of entry to the head centre. Upon this I
need not enlarge; all that I have taught you is re-

lated to the awakening of this highest centre, prior
to the aspirant's becoming a member of the Kingdom
of God. The ajna centre is *not* involved and it will
remain for several more centuries the agent of directed impression and not the objective of such
impressions.

The next key-thought which is of importance is found
in the words:

3. "The Plan is the dynamic *substance,* providing the
   content of the reservoir upon which the impressing
   agent can draw and to which the recipient of the
   impression must become sensitive."

This sentence requires probably a quite serious read-
justment in the thinking of most students. The concept of
the Plan as Substance will assuredly be new to them, and
new perhaps also to you. It is nevertheless a concept which
they must endeavour to grasp. Let me phrase it somewhat
differently: *The Plan constitutes or is composed of the substance in which the Members of the Hierarchy consistently
work.* Let us take this important concept and break it up
into its component parts for the sake of clarity. I am
strongly emphasising these words because this concept is of
an importance almost beyond human comprehension, and
because its understanding may revise and re-vitalise your
entire approach to the Plan, and you will therefore be enabled to work in a fresh and in an entirely new manner:

1. The Plan is substance. It is essentially substantial
   energy. And energy is substance and nothing else.
2. The substance (which is the Plan) is dynamic in nature, and is therefore impregnated with the energy
   of WILL.

3. The Plan constitutes a reservoir of energised substance, held in solution by the WILL of Sanat Kumara and *embodying* His intangible purpose (intangible to us but *not* intangible to Him).

4. It is this planetary Substance upon which the "impressing agents" must draw—the Nirmanakayas, the Members of the Hierarchy and the working disciples of the world, plus all spiritual sensitives of a certain degree.

5. Recipients of the desired impression must become sensitive to this substantial energy.

This entire proposition can be referred back to the originating Thinker Who brought our manifested world into being, and Who sequentially and under the Law of Evolution is bringing to fruition the objective of His thinking. In the larger and wider sense, it is that sumtotal of the ocean of energies in which "we live and move and have our being." This is the sevenfold body of the planetary Logos.

We are not here, however, considering the larger Whole, but *we are* dealing with a specific and focussed area of the planetary consciousness. This is found midway between the highest plane whereon the Council Chamber of the Great Lord is found and the three planes which form the active arena for hierarchical work—the three levels of consciousness of the Spiritual Triad. This "focussed area" has been precipitated by the Agents of the divine Will; They know the ultimate purpose of Sanat Kumara and hold it steadfastly in view, making it available to those Masters of the Wisdom Who can act as the "impressing Agents of Sanat Kumara's Will." These are the Manu, the Christ, and the Mahachohan, the Lord of Civilisation.

It might be said here that the three Buddhas of Activity are the prime impressing Agents and that the three Great

Lords are the "impressed Recipients" at an exceedingly high level; this is the atmic level of awareness, which is the area energised by the divine Will.

When dealing with the fifth Point of Revelation * I said that it concerned itself with the highest aspect of the Will—with that which produces the highest synthesis, the *final* synthesis. The planetary Purpose is the eventual synthesis of the initial thought of the planetary Logos, and to this thought we give always the unmeaning name of "GLORY"; this stands for all that we can conceive of the divine purpose; it is, for us, a "blaze of glory." The human mind is at this stage (in time and space) unable to register any aspect of the Purpose; all that we can do is to cooperate with the efforts of the Hierarchy to activate those things and events which will make the manifestation of the Purpose eventually possible. This purpose will constitute the ultimate revelation to the final root-race of men; it therefore lies a very long way ahead of our present point in evolution.

I will here make a statement which will probably convey nothing to the intelligence of the average disciple, but which may constitute a fruitful seed thought to the initiate who may read these words:

> *The Purpose of Sanat Kumara is created at present by the synthesis which the nature of the final seven Paths reveals. It is adapted in time and space to human intelligence by the presented Plan, and—in the glory of consummation—the completed Plan will reveal the Purpose on all the seven planes of evolution. Then evolution, as formulated and imposed by the Hierarchy, will end and a greater dynamic expansion will take its place.*

You will note that all along the lines of teaching there comes an eventual merging and blending, and that, at a

---

certain point in the development of consciousness, the many lines of spiritual approach become the few lines of conscious spiritual awareness. So it is in relation to the detail of the evolutionary process, with the formulation of the hierarchical Plan, and with the recognition of the Purpose. Speaking practically (and that is always of major importance), it might be said that evolution controls the *form* of the Purpose; the Plan concerns the hierarchical *recognition* of the Purpose, whilst the Purpose is the *synthetic Thought* which pours into the supernal consciousness of the Lord of the World along the seven Paths of which the Masters become aware at a certain very high initiation.

The seven great energies flow into our manifested world along the lines of the seven Paths; these are not the direct energies of the seven Rays, because these concern consciousness in a most specific manner; they are the substantial energies of material expression and their origin concerns a great mystery. These two lines of energy—material energy and the energy of consciousness—when brought together by divine Purpose, constitute the essential dualism of our manifested life.

All that we are able to recognise of that Purpose is the hierarchical Plan, and this only disciples and advanced aspirants can judge and recognise. This Plan is based upon knowledge of divine guidance in the Past, the recognition of progress out of that Past into the Present, plus the effort to become sensitive to the right emergence of that Plan (embodying ever an aspect of the Purpose) in the immediate Future. The Purpose is related to the Past, the Present and the Future; the Agents of the Plan are impressed from Shamballa, via the Nirmanakayas; the process is then repeated, and advanced humanity become the recipients, the sensitive recipients, of the Plan as transmitted to them by the impressing Agents, the Masters, working through the

New Group of World Servers. This group is the lower correspondence of the Nirmanakayas, the recipients of impression from Shamballa. See you, therefore, the beauty and the synthesis, the inter-dependence and the cooperative interplay which is demonstrated right through the chain of Hierarchy from the very highest Agent to the very lowest recipient of divine impression.

The key to all this is energy. Energy is substance, and this substance is qualified by divine dynamic WILL. There is much to be learnt anent the Will. Will as dynamic energy is not yet understood in its true sense by human beings. Mankind usually recognises will as fixed determination; this is in reality their individual effort to impress substance (personal or environing) with their own self-will or with their well-intended effort to conform to what they believe to be the will of God, speaking symbolically. But men know nothing yet of the process of *working with* dynamic energised substance, for it basically impresses them and uses them as they become aware of the Plan and thus come under the influence of the Spiritual Triad. They are used and not using that which is available for the furtherance of the Plan—the dynamic energy of the divine Will. This dynamic Will cannot become available nor can disciples truly work with the Plan *until* the antahkarana is to some measure adequately constructed, though not yet perfected.

It becomes of service, therefore, for the aspirant and the disciple to know the nature of the Agents Who can locate their magnetic aura and impress upon it Their understanding of the Plan; these Agents may be accepted disciples or initiates and Masters; then the aspirant or disciple must find those to whom he can personally act as an impressing agent. He has consequently to study himself as *a recipient* and also as *an agent,* as a responsive factor and also as an originating and impressing factor. This might be regarded as the scientific approach to the spiritual life, and it is of value because the necessity of service is implicit in the necessity for receptivity; all is, therefore, related to Invocation and Evocation.

It is in our next basic theme, the nature of the etheric body, that we shall find again the higher relationships and the interdependence of many allied factors. This interdependence emerges acutely the higher one progresses into the scheme of correspondences. Eventually, a point of fusion is reached.

The subject of the etheric body of all forms and of the etheric body of the planetary Logos is necessarily of major importance in any consideration of the *Supreme Science of Contact*. It is this concept of sensitive contact which I seek to emphasise as we study the three points or the three basic concepts outlined in the preceding section. All such terms as planes, groups, creative Hierarchies, and centres are simply word modes of inferring relationship, interplay and mutual impression between the beings or the lives who make up the sumtotal of our manifested universe; they are nevertheless signs of our leading up to a planetary synthesis or a planetary integrity of a nature hitherto not even visioned by man.

The subject is necessarily one of immense difficulty, for all human beings think in terms of their own contacts and relationships, which are strictly limited and are not expressed in terms of the One Life, flowing through all forms and all kingdoms, or through all the diverse planetary evolutions (of which you know nothing) and thus creating in time and space a living intelligent planetary Entity of systemic maturity, qualified by immense attractive and integrating energies, motivated by a supreme Purpose—a Purpose which is part of the vast purpose of the solar Logos, working through the planetary Logoi, and therefore responsible for the well-being and progressive evolution of all lives and groups of lives within the framework and the essential structure of our planet.

The relation evoked is, as you can well imagine, inter-planetary and extra-planetary; these terms mean little to the average disciple and he has to wait until the initiatory process puts him in a position where he can frankly evaluate the situation. Of the latter stages, we can know nothing; only in the Council Chamber of Shamballa are these extra-planetary contacts and relationships recognisable. But one basic fact must be grasped, and that is that the medium of relationship and of contact is SUBSTANCE; and the effect of these relationships, carried on through this medium, is the gradual development and progressive unfoldment of the three divine Aspects which all esotericists recognise, and of others which the coming millenia will reveal. The contributing factor, therefore, within and upon our planet is what we might regard as the three major centres of the planetary Logos:

1. *The Head Centre,* the dynamic Agent of the extra-planetary Purpose, the expression of the divine planetary Will as focussed in Shamballa. This is the energy of Synthesis, the source of all planetary life; it connotes essential Being.
2. *The Heart Centre,* the Agent of the Plan of evolution. This is the expression of divine Love or pure Reason, the Hierarchy. It is essentially the energy of Attraction, the kingdom of souls.
3. *The Throat Centre,* the Agent of all the three Aspects in relation to the three subhuman kingdoms in nature, the expression also of the divine Intelligence, Humanity. This is the energy of active Mind and makes humanity the macrocosm of the micro-cosm, the three subhuman kingdoms. Humanity is to these kingdoms what the Hierarchy is to the fourth kingdom in nature, the human kingdom.

These are the elements of the occult science and—for students such as you—contain nothing new. Nevertheless, they need to be seen in their triple relationship if the mode of working of the One Life is to be grasped more clearly than is now the case. The aim of the entire evolutionary scheme is to bring these three Centres into such a close relationship that the synthesis of the divine Purpose can work out harmoniously on every possible (note that phrase) level of consciousness. If this can take place, then the basic Thought, the fundamental Proposition of the planetary Logos can eventually be disclosed to man.

May I remind you of the occult statement that every living being or manifested life—from the planetary Logos down to the tiniest atom—either has been, is, or will be a man. This has reference to the past, to the present and to the future of every manifested life. Therefore, the fact of humanity and of that for which humanity stands is probably the primary and major aspect of the divine purpose. Pause and think about this statement. It is, therefore, the first clear fact which indicates the measure and the magnitude of a human being; and until two other facts are sequentially revealed to us, it will not be possible correctly to gauge the wider aspects of the purpose of Sanat Kumara. Everything subhuman is slowly moving towards a definite human experience; it is also passing through the phase of human effort and consequent experience, or else it has moved out of that phase of limitation and—through initiation—is drafting human nature into a state of divinity (to use a most inadequate phrase).

The keynote, therefore, of the Lord of the World is HUMANITY for it is the basis, the goal and the essential inner structure of all being. Humanity itself is the key to all evolutionary processes and to all correct understanding of the divine Plan, expressing in time and space the divine Purpose. Why HE chose that this should be so, we know not; but it is a point to be accepted and remembered in all study of the Science of Impression because it is the factor that makes relationship and contact possible and it is also the source of all understanding. These are most difficult things to express and to enlarge upon, my brothers, and only the penetrating intuition can make these matters clearer to your avid and active intelligence.

You will note, therefore, that though we call one of the major centres HUMANITY, yet—in the last analysis—all the centres are constituted of lives progressing towards the human stage, of those units of life who are at the human stage, and those who have left that stage far behind but who are endowed with all the faculties and all the knowledges wrought out into human expression in earlier planetary schemes or solar systems, or through our own definite and characteristic planetary life.

Because of this uniformity of experience, the art of contact and the science of impression become entirely possible and normally effective. The great and omnipotent Lives in Shamballa can impress the omniscient Lives and lesser lives in the Hierarchy *because* They share a common humanity; the hierarchical Workers or Masters and Initiates can consequently impress humanity because of shared experience and understanding; then the lives that compose the human family present the goal to the subhuman kingdoms and can, and do, impress them because of basic instinctual tendencies which are expressed in the human group but which are latent instinctual tendencies and potential assets in the three subhuman groups.

This teaching has always been implicit in the esoteric doctrines but has not been sufficiently emphasised, owing to the point in evolution of mankind. Today, mankind has made such progress that these points can be made effectively. I would call to your attention that this was the keynote of the Gospel story: the human-divine nature of the Christ, relating Him to the Father through His essential divinity, and also to man through His essential humanity. The Christian Church gave a wrong slant to the teaching by making Christ appear as unique, though the higher criticism (deemed so shocking fifty years ago) has done much to correct this false impression.

The outstanding characteristic of humanity is intelligent sensitivity to impression. Ponder on this definite and emphatic statement. The work of science is, after all, simply the development of the knowledge of substance and of form; this knowledge will make it possible for humanity eventually to act as the major impressing agent in relation to the three subhuman kingdoms in nature; that is humanity's primary responsibility. This work of relationship is practically the work of developing or the mode of unfoldment of human sensitivity. I refer here to sensitivity to impression from or by the Hierarchy.

The work done through the processes of initiation is intended to fit disciples and initiates to receive impression from Shamballa; the initiate is essentially a blend of scientific and religious training; he has been re-oriented to certain phases of divine existence which are not yet recognised by the average human being. I am endeavouring to make clear to you the basic synthesis underlying all manifested life upon our planet, and also the close interplay or relationship which forever exists and expresses itself through the supreme science of contact or of impression.

The three great Centres are in close relationship at all times, even if this is not yet recognised by the intelligent disciple; an unbroken series of impressions is ever present, relating one centre to another and bringing about an evolutionary unity of objective, and developing (with exceeding rapidity at this time) a secondary science, that of Invocation and Evocation. This science is in reality the science of impression in activity and not simply in theory.

The first great *Invocation* was uttered by the planetary Logos when He expressed the desire to manifest and thus invoked and brought to Himself the substance needed for His designed expression. That started the chain of being or of hierarchy; inter-relation was then set up between all "substantial" units; the more potent and the more dynamic and greater could then impress the lesser and the weaker until gradually—as the aeons swept by—the seven Centres were created and were in close impressionable relationship. Of these seven we are at this time considering only three; the others we know very little about, for they are largely composed of units of the deva evolutions (and I would ask you to note the plurality there) and of subhuman lives, working under impression from the head, the heart and the throat centres of the planetary Logos.

Students are apt to make their thinking unduly complicated when they seek to itemise and define, to separate into academic groups and brackets the multiplicity of energies with which they feel confronted when considering the planetary and the human centres. I would advise you that you think simply and (certainly, at first) in terms of the three major energies as they emanate from some centre, become impressing agents, and then are again transmitted or stepped down:

1. *The dynamic electrical energy of Life itself* or divine potency, of embodied Purpose, expressing through evolutionary manifestation the divine Will. It might be well to realise that *purpose* emanates from the cosmic mental plane and is the all-inclusive, synthetic, motivating principle which expresses itself as the divine will upon the cosmic physical plane—the seven planes of our planetary Life. This dynamic energy focuses itself through the Lives or Beings

Who control and dominate Shamballa. Until the divine purpose has been achieved, the planetary Logos holds all in manifestation through the potency of His Will, and animates all forms with electric fire. Knowledge of this Will and Purpose comes to the student who is constructing the antahkarana and who is, therefore, coming under the control of the Spiritual Triad, the threefold expression of the Monad.

2. *The attractive magnetic solar energy* to which we give the quite unsuitable name of Love. It is this energy which constitutes the cohering, unifying force which holds the manifested universe or planetary form together and is responsible for all relationships; it is this energy which is the soul of all things or of all forms, beginning with the anima mundi and reaching its highest point of expression in the human soul which is the constituent factor in the fifth kingdom in nature, the Kingdom of God or of Souls. An understanding of this human potency comes as a man makes contact with his own soul and sets up a stable relationship with that soul; then he becomes a soul-infused personality. As you well know, the threefold personality is to the soul what the Spiritual Triad is to the Monad: a clear medium of expression. Most students are or should be today occupied with this attractive energy, for until they have mastered the desire nature and have transmuted it into aspiration and soul control, they cannot hope to comprehend the dynamic energy of electric fire. This attractive magnetism is the energy dominating and controlling the Hierarchy.

3. *The intelligent activity of fire by friction.* Students would be well advised to re-read *A Treatise on Cosmic Fire* where I deal at length with these three conditioning energies. This third energy is the basic energy expressing itself in the three worlds and in the four kingdoms in nature, climaxing its expression in the creative energy of the human kingdom.

This energy emanated originally (as far as our solar system and our planetary scheme are concerned) in the first solar system and is the best proven and the best known energy in manifestation. It is the medium for activity in all forms through which the planetary Logos expresses Himself; it is the result of the activity of the divine Mind, as that peculiar type of divine energy plays upon and through all atoms and upon all atomic forms. The fission of the nucleus of the atom in the past few years is the outer sign or demonstration that humanity has "encompassed" the divine Mind and can now move on to "encompass" the love or the attractive nature of divinity. Ponder upon this statement. I know not what word to use but *encompass* and it is entirely inadequate. A new and deeper esoteric terminology is badly needed.

If you will work with and reflect upon these three fundamental energies and search for their expression within yourself, you will greatly simplify your occult thinking. Let me here make a few more statements which you have perforce to accept hypothetically, but which can nevertheless be substantiated by you if you arrive at an understanding of the Law of Analogy or of Correspondences, and if you will also accept the truism that the microcosm reflects the macrocosm and, therefore, each human being is related to Deity through *essential similarity*.

Statement One.

Dynamic electric energy entered into our planetary sphere from extra-planetary sources and from a point of definite focus upon the cosmic mental plane; this energy was paralleled by a secondary energy from the sun Sirius, thus accounting for the dualism of manifestation.

Statement Two.

This energy expanded outward from its central focus (the centre called Shamballa) and in this expansion became the agency which *impressed* the Plan upon the serving Hierarchy. The Plan is that measure of possibility of immediate importance which the divine Purpose can present at any given moment in time and space.

Statement Three.

This process of expansion set up another focal point of energy, and the heart centre of the planet, the Hierarchy came into being; thus two centres were created and en rapport, which constitutes a major event upon the involutionary arc; to this, little attention has hitherto been paid. It coincided with the advent or the arrival of the Lords of Flame from the alter ego of our Earth, the planet Venus. They created the nucleus of the Hierarchy which—in that far, very distant time—consisted of only forty-nine members; these were advanced human beings and not souls awaiting incarnation in human form on Earth, as was the case with the vast majority of these visiting Solar Angels.

Statement Four.

Alignment between the head centre and the heart centre upon the involutionary arc was thus set up; another expansion took place which resulted, as you know well, in the creation of a new kingdom in nature, the fourth or human kingdom. This kingdom was destined to become and is today the third major centre in the planetary life. Then another alignment, but one which is still contained upon the involutionary arc, took place.

Statement Five.

Today, an evolutionary alignment is taking place. The planetary centre which we call Humanity is active and vibrant, and it is now possible to "progress along the Upward Way and create the line which links the lesser with the higher, permitting thus an interplay." Men are rapidly moving out of the human centre into the hierarchical centre; the mass of men *are* responding to spiritual impression.

Statement Six.

At the same time, the heart centre of the planetary Logos, the Hierarchy, whilst it is being responsive to the invocation of the throat centre, Humanity, is becoming increasingly evocative and is itself attaining a much higher contact and alignment with the head centre of the planetary Logos; it is, therefore, capable of receiving a constantly developing dynamic *impression* from Shamballa.

Statement Seven.

Thus a great alignment is being achieved through the relationship and the interplay going on between these three major planetary centres; this produces a constant inflow of energies from several different sources, and these energies galvanise these three centres into a new and increased activity. Invocation is arising all the time between these centres and producing a consequent evocation of impressing energies.

In these seven statements, you have depicted a PATTERN of the present planetary work or the present logoic thesis. An involutionary alignment (the guarantee of future successful alignments) constitutes most ancient history; an evolutionary alignment in which all three centres are involved is constantly producing an interplay of energies as well as a constantly successful impression of one centre upon another. Humanity, as the throat centre of the planetary Logos and the prime planetary creative agency (which modern science demonstrates), invokes the heart centre, the Hierarchy, and then receives the needed impression which will result in the developing civilisations and cultures as well as the eventual appearance on Earth of the fifth or spiritual kingdom. The Hierarchy or the planetary heart centre invokes Shamballa, the planetary head centre, and the Plan—as an expression of the Purpose—is impressed upon the hierarchical consciousness. If there is redundancy in these various comments of mine, it is entirely intentional; repetition serves the purposes of accurate presentation where esotericism is concerned.

As the invocative system spreads and a greater alignment is attained, Shamballa—the planetary head centre—invokes energies outside the planetary life and the inflow of cosmic and solar energies will be very much greater; for this the esotericists of the world must be prepared. It will also produce the advent or appearance of many AVATARS, bringing with Them many and very different kinds of energies to those which hitherto have controlled human affairs and the events and evolution of the other, the subhuman kingdoms in nature. With the reappearance of the Christ as the focal point or the supreme Agent of the planetary heart centre, a new era or "divine epoch" will be instituted. The Avatar of Synthesis will draw very close to humanity and He will inaugurate the "reign of Avatars" Who will be embodied Purpose and spiritual Will; They will initiate both the Hierarchy and Humanity into phases of the divine character of which, at present, nothing is known and for which we have no terminology that could convey the exact facts and nature. All that I am attempting to do here is to give you a general outline of events which may lie centuries ahead but which will inevitably occur—once the Christ is again in physical Presence and recognition on Earth.

H.P.B. speaks in *The Secret Doctrine* of the "three periodical vehicles," referring as he does so to the Monad, the Soul and the Personality; he is dealing, therefore, with the nine aspects of divinity which connote the nine major initiations and those divine characteristics through which the three major aspects of divinity reflect themselves. In this connection, it is well known to students that the Monad expresses itself through the Spiritual Triad, the Soul through the three aspects of the Egoic Lotus, and the Personality through the three mechanical vehicles. It will be obvious to you surely that these three periodical vehicles are under the influence or impression of the three major planetary centres and are, therefore, finally conditioned by the three major energies to which I referred earlier in this section. I do not feel it to be necessary to enlarge upon this basic relation; it is that which integrates the human soul into the vast general whole and makes the individual an intrinsic part of the sumtotal.

There is one aspect of the *Science of Impression* upon which I have not yet touched and that is the place of the centres as focal points, as transmitters or as agencies for the seven ray energies. It is known to esotericists that each of the seven centres comes under the influence or is the recipient of some ray energy, and there is a general acceptance of the fact that the head centre is the agent of the first Ray of Will or Power, the heart centre is the custodian of second Ray energy of Love-Wisdom, whilst the third Ray of active creative Intelligence passes through and energises the throat centre. These Rays of Aspect do find expression through the three centres above the diaphragm, and—on the larger scale—through Shamballa, the Hierarchy and Humanity. It is, however, equally true that Shamballa is primarily second ray as it is expressed, because that is the ray of the present solar system of which Shamballa is a part; and that the first ray, or its dynamic life aspect, is focused in the heart, for the heart is the centre of life. The great centre which we call Humanity is predominantly governed by the third Ray of Active Intelligence. This ray energy arrives at the throat centre via the head and the heart centres. I am pointing this out for two reasons which must form part of your thinking as you study this science:

1. All the centres come under the influence of all the rays, and this must surely be obvious in relation to average and undeveloped human beings. Were this not so, such human beings would be unable to respond to first ray, second ray and third ray energy, for the centres above the diaphragm are, in their case, inactive.

2. In time and space and during the evolutionary process, it is not possible to say which centre is expressing the energy of any particular ray, for there is a constant movement and activity. The centre at the base of the spine is frequently the expression of first ray energies. This is apt to be confusing. The human mind seeks to make everything precise, stable, to bracket certain relations or to assign certain centres to certain ray energies. This cannot be done.

At the end of the world cycle, when divine purpose is fulfilled and the evolutionary process has brought about the changes and adjustments needed for the full expression of the Will of Sanat Kumara, then the situation will be different and men will know (as the Members of the Hierarchy know) which centres express the seven ray energies. It must be remembered also that the Rays of Attribute shift and change constantly; for instance, humanity as the planetary throat centre is under the constant influence of the seventh ray, as is the solar plexus centre of the planet. To that subdiaphragmatic centre I give no name. Though the human throat centre is primarily expressing the third ray, there is an interesting situation to be noted in this connection: two ray energies control this centre *at this time.*

The throat centre of the average integrated personality is governed by the third ray and is strongly energised by third ray energies (again seven in number), whilst the throat centre of the spiritual aspirant, of disciples and initiates below the third initiation is responding primarily to seventh ray influence, and this is peculiarly the case now as the seventh ray is in incarnation. The rays which are manifesting at any particular time affect powerfully all the other centres as well as the one through which they are normally expressing. This is a point oft forgotten.

It is needless for me to point out that—as man progresses upon the Path of Return—he consistently comes under the impression of the centre of which he is an integral part: that is, first of all, the planetary throat centre, the human family; then, as a soul, he comes under the impression of the Hierarchy, the planetary heart centre, and at that point he begins to express the combined energies of the intelligence and of love; finally, on the Path of Initiation, he comes under the impression of Shamballa, the planetary head centre, and becomes a participant in the divine Purpose and an Agent of the divine Plan.

It is therefore literally and eternally true that the same energetic Life pours through the planetary centres, into and through the three periodical vehicles of the incarnated Monad, and finally into and through the three centres in the human etheric body which correspond to the three major centres of the planetary Logos. There is, therefore, nowhere to be found any basis for separation or any possible point of separation or of essential division. Any sense of separateness is due simply to ignorance and to the fact that certain energies are as yet unable to make adequate impression upon the human consciousness, functioning in time and space. The essential synthesis exists and the end is sure and inevitable; unity *is* attainable because unity exists and the sense of separateness is simply the Great Illusion.

It was in order to hasten the dispelling of this great illusion of separateness in the minds of men, and to bring about the emergence of the basic existing unity, that the new world prayer was given to men and its use on a world wide scale inaugurated. Elsewhere * I have told you of the origin and the impulsing of the Great Invocation. Here I am simply placing it before you as a fitting conclusion to this portion of my labour of love in the presentation of truth, and as a possible starting point in yours.

From the point of Light within the Mind of God
 Let light stream forth into the minds of men.
  Let Light descend on Earth.

From the point of Love within the Heart of God
 Let love stream forth into the hearts of men.
  May Christ return to Earth.

From the centre where the Will of God is known
 Let purpose guide the little wills of men—
  The purpose which the Masters know and serve.

From the centre which we call the race of men
 Let the Plan of Love and Light work out
  And may it seal the door where evil dwells.

Let Light and Love and Power restore the Plan on Earth

---

* *The Reappearance of the Christ.*

TEACHING ON THE ETHERIC VEHICLE

I. THE NATURE OF THE ETHERIC BODY

Much that I may say here may be familiar to a certain extent, because there is a vast amount of information anent the etheric body scattered throughout my various books. It will have its value however if students can receive in a few pages a general idea and the basic concepts which underlie the teaching—or should I say, the fact? If they have the time, students would find it of profit to re-read what I said; run their eyes rapidly through the books and papers in search of the word "etheric." They will never regret it. Life itself, the training to be given in the future, the conclusions of science and a new mode of civilisation will all increasingly be focussed on this unique substance which is the true form to which all physical bodies in every kingdom in nature conform. Note that phraseology.

The attitude of occultism is, at this time, relatively negative to the fact and the nature of the etheric body. People are ready to admit its existence, but the dominant factors in their consciousness are the fact of the physical body (around whose comfort, security and care all life seems woven) and the fact of the astral or emotional nature. Not one among them, or among occult students generally, pays any attention to the etheric body, and there is a great hiatus or gap in consciousness today (only this time normally and rightly) between the personality and the Spiritual Triad. This gap will be bridged by the building of the antahkarana, and this can only be built by advanced students. There is no such planned bridge for the gap in

NOTE: See Chart *Evolution of a Solar Logos,* p. xi.

consciousness between the physical body and the etheric counterpart. The etheric body exists in subtle etheric matter, and factually there is no true gap; there is simply the ignoring by humanity of an aspect of the physical body which is of far more importance than is the dense physical vehicle. The consciousness of men today is physical-astral, and the factor of conditioning energies is ignored, over-looked, and—from the angle of consciousness—non-existent.

One of the main obligations of occult students today is to testify to the fact of the etheric body; modern science is already thus testifying because its researches have now landed it in the realm of energy. Electro-therapy, the growing recognition that man is electrical in nature, and the realisation that even the atom in apparently inanimate objects is a living vibrant entity substantiate this occult point of view. Generally speaking, science has preceded esotericism in its recognition of energy as a dominant factor in all form expression. Theosophists and others pride themselves on being ahead of human thinking, but such is not the case. H. P. B., an initiate of high standing, presented views ahead of science, but that does not apply to the exponents of the theosophical teaching. The fact of all manifested forms being forms of energy, and that the true human form is no exception, is the gift of science to humanity and not the gift of occultism. The demonstration that light and matter are synonymous terms is also a scientific conclusion. Esotericists have always known this, but their aggressive and foolish presentations of the truth have greatly handicapped the Hierarchy. Frequently the Masters have deplored the technique of the theosophists and other occult groups. When the new presentation of the occult teaching made its appearance through the inspired activity of H. P. B., a number (an increasing number as the years slipped by) of theosophical members presented the occult teaching in such a manner that it travestied the true teaching and outraged the intellectual perception of the mass of enquiring and intelligent men. The teaching on the etheric body is an instance of this. H. P. B. was largely responsible, because of utilising the word "astral" to cover a mass of information anent the etheric as well as the astral. This was due to the realisation of the fact that the astral body was doomed in a few generations (relatively speaking) to disappear, and for H. P. B. in particular was already non-existent, owing to the advanced point in evolution reached by this disciple.

Realising that the etheric body was an expression always of the dominant energy controlling mankind in any particular cycle, H. P. B. used the term "astral body" as interchangeable with the etheric body. The etheric body, in the vast majority of cases is the vehicle or the instrument of astral energy. The mass of men are still Atlantean or astral in their natures, and this means a far larger percentage than the average occultist is willing to admit. H. P. B. was, however, truthful and knew that at that time and for several hundred years afterwards (probably about three hundred years) the astral body would continue to govern the mass of human reactions and their consequent daily life expression. Hence the apparent confusion in the writings between these two "bodies."

Here is a basic statement—one that is so basic that it governs and controls all thinking anent the etheric body:

> *The etheric body is primarily composed of the dominant energy or energies to which the man, the group, the nation, or the world reacts in any particular time cycle or world period.*

If you are to understand clearly, it is essential that I lay down certain propositions anent the etheric body which should govern all the student's thinking; if they do not, he will be approaching the truth from the wrong angle; this, modern science does not do. The limitation of modern science is its lack of vision; the hope of modern science is that it does recognise truth when proven. Truth in all circumstances is essential and in this matter science gives a desirable lead, even though it ignores and despises occultism. Occult scientists handicap themselves either because of their presentation of the truth or because of a false humility. Both are equally bad.

There are six major propositions which govern all consideration of the etheric body, and I would like to present them to students as a first step:

1. There is nothing in the manifested universe—solar, planetary or the various kingdoms in nature—which does not possess an energy form, subtle and intangible yet substantial, which controls, governs and conditions the outer physical body. This is the etheric body.

2. This energy form—underlying the solar system, the planets and all forms within their specific rings-pass-not—is itself conditioned and governed by the dominant solar or planetary energy which ceaselessly and without break in time, creates it, changes and qualifies it. The etheric body is subject to ceaseless change. This, being true of the Macrocosm, is equally true of man, the microcosm, and—through the agency of humanity—will eventually and mysteriously prove true of all the subhuman kingdoms in nature. Of this, the animal kingdom and the vegetable kingdom are already evidences.

3. The etheric body is composed of interlocking and circulating lines of force emanating from one or

other, or from one or many, of the seven planes or areas of consciousness of our planetary Life.

4. These lines of energy and this closely interlocking system of streams of force are related to seven focal points or centres to be found within the etheric body. These centres are related, each of them, to certain types of incoming energy. When the energy reaching the etheric body is not related to a particular centre, then that centre remains quiescent and unawakened; when it is related and the centre is sensitive to its impact, then that centre becomes vibrant and receptive and develops as a controlling factor in the life of the man on the physical plane.

5. The dense physical body, composed of atoms—each with its own individual life, light and activity—is held together by and is expressive of the energies which compose the etheric body. These, as will be apparent, are of two natures:

   a. The energies which form (through interlocked "lines of forceful energy") the underlying etheric body, as a whole and in relation to all physical forms. This form is qualified then by the *general* life and vitality of the plane on which the Dweller in the body functions, and therefore where his consciousness is normally focussed.

   b. The particularised or specialised energies by which the individual (at this particular point in evolution, through the circumstances of his daily life and his heredity) *chooses* to govern his daily activities.

6. The etheric body has many centres of force, responsive to the manifold energies of our planetary Life, but we shall consider only the seven major

centres which respond to the inflowing energies of the seven rays. All lesser centres are conditioned by the seven major centres; this is a point which students are apt to forget. It is here that knowledge of the egoic and of the personality rays is of prime usefulness.

It can be seen, therefore, how exceedingly important this subject of energy becomes, because it controls and makes the man what he is at any given moment, and likewise indicates the plane on which he should function, and the method whereby he should govern his environment, circumstances and relationships. If this is grasped by him, it will enable him to realise that he will have to shift his whole attention from the physical or the astral planes on to the etheric levels of awareness; his objective will then be to determine what energy should control his daily expression (or energies, if he is an advanced disciple). He will realise also that as his attitude, attainment and comprehension shift to ever higher levels, his etheric body will be constantly changing and responding to the newer energies. These energies he will be *will-fully* bringing in; this is the right use of the word "will-full."

It is not easy for the average seer or clairvoyant to distinguish the etheric body from its environment or to isolate its particular type of energy or livingness, for the reason that its automaton, the physical body—being composed of vibrant energetic atoms—is itself in constant movement, and such movement involves a necessary radiation as a consequence; animal magnetism is an illustration of this radiation. This emanation from the dense physical body normally and naturally mingles with the energies of the etheric body, and thus only the trained seer can differentiate between the two, particularly within the physical body itself.

From one point of view the etheric body can be looked at in two ways: first, as it interpenetrates, underlies and occupies the entire physical organism and, secondly, as it extends beyond the physical form and surrounds it like an aura. According to the point in evolution will be the extent of the area which the etheric body covers beyond the outside of the physical body. It may extend for a few or many inches. It is only in this area that the vital body can be studied with relative ease, once the emanatory activity of the physical atoms is offset or allowed for.

Within the physical body, the network of the etheric body is to be found permeating every single part. It is peculiarly associated at this time with the nervous system, which is fed, nourished, controlled and galvanised by its etheric counterpart. This counterpart is present in millions of tiny streams or lines of energy, to which the Eastern occultist has given the name "nadis." These nadis are the carriers of energy. They are in fact the energy itself and carry the quality of energy from some area of consciousness in which the "dweller in the body" may happen to be focused. This may be the astral plane or the planes of the Spiritual Triad, for none of the energies can control the physical body from any plane, no matter how high, except in this manner. According to the focus of the consciousness, the psychic state of awareness, the potency of aspiration or desire, and the point in evolution or the spiritual status, so will be the type of energy carried by the nadis, passing from them to the outer nervous system. This general proposition must be accepted, for the whole subject is as yet too intricate, and the mechanism of observation of the student too undeveloped, for me to enter into greater detail. This will suffice as an initial hypothesis upon which to work.

The amount of energy and the type of energy controlling any aspect of the nervous system is conditioned by the centre in its immediate area. A centre is a distributing agency, in the last analysis. Even though that energy will affect the entire body, the centre most responsive to the quality and type will potently affect the nadis, and therefore the nerves, in its immediate environment.

It must always be remembered that the seven centres are *not* within the dense physical body. They exist *only* in etheric matter and in the etheric so-called aura, outside the physical body. They are closely related to the dense physical body by the network of nadis. Five of the centres are to be found in the etheric counterpart of the spinal column, and the energy passes (through large and responsive nadis) through the vertebrae of the spine and circulates then throughout the etheric body as it is interiorly active within the physical vehicle. The three head centres exist, one just above the top of the head, another just in front of the eyes and forehead, and the third at the back of the head, just above where the spinal column ends. This makes eight centres but is in reality seven, as the centre at the back of the head is not counted in the initiation process, any more than is the spleen.

The powerful effect of the inflow of energy, via the energy body, has itself automatically created these centres or these reservoirs of force, these focal points of energy, which the spiritual man must learn to use and through the means of which he can direct energy where needed. Each of these seven centres has appeared in the course of human evolution in response to energy from one or other, or from several, of the seven rays. The impact of these rays upon the etheric body, emanating as they do periodically and ceaselessly from the seven rays, is so potent that the seven areas in the etheric body become more highly sensitised than the rest of the vehicle, and these in due time develop into responsive distributing centres. The effect of these seven centres upon the physical body in due time produces a condensation or a state of what is called "attracted response" from dense matter, and thus the seven major sets of endocrine glands slowly came into functioning activity. It must here be remembered that the whole development of the etheric body falls into two historical stages:

1. That in which the etheric energy, flowing through responsive centres and creating the endocrine glands as a consequence, gradually began to have a definite effect upon the blood stream; the energy worked through that medium solely for a very long time. This still remains true, for the life aspect of energy animates the blood, through the medium of the centres and their agents, the glands. Hence the words in the Bible that "the blood is the life."

2. As the race of men developed, and consciousness grew greater and certain great expansions took place, the centres began to extend their usefulness and to use the nadis, and thus to work upon and through the nervous system; this produced conscious and planned activity upon the physical plane, commensurate to the man's place in evolution.

Thus the incoming energy forming the etheric body created a needed etheric mechanism with its corresponding dense physical counterparts; it therefore, as will be noted from its relationship to the blood via the glands, and to the nervous system via the nadis (both through the medium of the seven centres), became the transmitter of two aspects of energy: one of which was kama-manasic (desire-lower mind) and the other atmic-buddhic (spiritual will—spiritual love) in the case of advanced humanity. Herein lies full opportunity for all, as the Law of Evolution proceeds to dominate all manifestation. What is true of the Macrocosm is true also of the microcosm.

The use of the creative imagination is of value here. It may not give a true picture on all points, but it will convey one great reality. The reality to which I refer is that there is no possible separateness in our manifested planetary life—or elsewhere for that matter, even beyond our planetary ring-pass-not. The concept of separateness, of individual isolation, is an illusion of the unillumined human mind. Everything—every form, every organism within all forms, all aspects of manifested life in every kingdom in nature—is intimately related each to each through the planetary etheric body (of which all etheric bodies are integral parts) which substands all that is. Little as it may mean, and useless as it may appear, the table at which you write, the flower you hold in your hand, the horse on which you ride, the man to whom you talk, are sharing with you the vast circulatory life of the planet as it streams into, through and out of every aspect of the form nature. The only differences which exist are those in consciousness, and peculiarly so in the consciousness of man and of the Black Lodge. There is only the ONE LIFE, pouring through the mass of forms which, in their sumtotal, constitute our planet—as we know it.

All forms are related, inter-related and interdependent; the planetary etheric body holds them together so that a cohesive, coherent, expressive Whole is presented to the eye of man, or one great unfolding consciousness to the perception of the Hierarchy. Lines of light pass from form to form. Some are bright and some are dim; some move or circulate with rapidity, others are lethargic and slow in their interplay; some seem to circulate with facility in some particular kingdom in nature and some in another; some come from one direction and some from a different one, but all are in movement all the time; it is a constant circulation. All are passing on and into and through, and there is not one single atom in the body which is not the recipient of this living, moving energy; there is no single form that is not "kept in shape and livingness" by this determined inflow and outflow, and there is therefore no part of the body of manifestation (which is an integral part of the planetary vehicle of the Lord of the World) which is not in complex but complete touch with HIS divine intention—through the medium of HIS three major centres: Shamballa, the Hierarchy, and Humanity. In the multiplicity of the forms of which His great composite vehicle is composed, there is no need for Him to be in conscious touch. It is, however, possible, should He so desire it, but it would profit Him not, any more than it would profit you to be in conscious touch with some atom in some organ of your physical body. He works, however, through His three major centres: Shamballa, the planetary head centre; the Hierarchy, the planetary heart centre; and Humanity, the planetary throat centre. The play of the energies elsewhere (controlled from these three centres) is automatic. The objective of the circulating energies—as it appears to us when we seek to penetrate divine purpose—is to vivify all parts of His body, with the view of promoting the unfoldment of consciousness therein.

This is basically true from the angle of Shamballa "where the Will of God is known"; it is partially true of those Members of the Hierarchy Who sense the Purpose and formulate the Plan and then present it in an understandable form to the lesser initiates and disciples and aspirants. These two groups work entirely on the consciousness side, which motivates and directs (as needed) the moving, circulating energies. This is not true of the bulk of humanity, who are conscious but only conscious within their ring-pass-not, and are therefore fundamentally separated off by their emphasis upon form as it exists in the three worlds—the dense physical levels of the cosmic physical plane. On the lowest of these levels, the outer physical form reacts and responds to the circulating energies through the medium of the etheric energy which comes from the lowest of the four levels of the etheric plane.

Gradually the consciousness within these forms reacts to the nature of the outer vehicle as it is impulsed from etheric levels, and a profoundly significant development takes place. This development—to make a wide generalisation—falls into three categories:

1. The outer form changes under the impact of the etheric energies entering in, passing through and disappearing from (ceaselessly aeon after aeon) the form. The energy that is there one minute is gone the next.
2. This ceaseless play of energy varies in time and space, and moves lethargically, rapidly or rhythmically according to the type or nature of the form through which it is at any moment passing.
3. The energy of the etheric plane changes considerably as the aeons pass away, according to the direction or the source from which it comes. The directing energy alters significantly as evolution proceeds.

Students have been apt to speak simply of the etheric body as an entire integral entity and as constituted solely of etheric substance, forgetting that the etheric body is the medium for the transfer of many types of energy. They forget the following facts:

1. That the etheric body is itself composed of four types of substance, each of which is definitely specialised and found on one or other of the etheric levels.

2. That these substances, functioning actively in any particular etheric body, create a network of channels; they produce fine tubes (if I may use so inappropriate a word) which take the general form of the dense material or tangible form with which they may be associated. This form underlies every part of the physical body and can be seen extending for a certain distance outside of the recognisable form. This etheric body is not in reality an ovoid (as the older occult books teach) but usually takes the form or general outline of the physical vehicle with which it is associated. When, however, the head centre is awakened and functioning, then the ovoid appearance is far more frequent.

3. These channels or tubes—according to the type of energy they carry—pass to certain areas of the body, via three main stations:

    a. The seven major centres, of which you have heard much.
    b. The twenty-one minor centres, which I outlined for you earlier.*
    c. The forty-nine focal points, scattered all over the body.

4. All these centres and focal points for the transmission of energy are connected each with each by larger channels than the mass of channels which constitute the etheric body as a whole, because many lesser channels and lines of force or energy merge and blend as they near a centre or a focal point.

---

* *A Treatise on the Seven Rays,* Volume IV, (pp. 72-73).

5. The mass of the smaller channels or the channeling tubes of energy eventually create in all forms that layer of corresponding nerves which are not yet recognised by medical science but which are like an intermediary web or network. These relate the etheric body as a whole to the entire two-fold nervous system (cerebro-spinal and the sympathetic nervous systems) which science does recognise. It is this system underlying the nerves which is the true response apparatus and which—via the brain—telegraphs information to the mind or, via the brain and the mind, keeps the soul informed. It is this system of nadis which is used in full consciousness by the initiate who has related the Spiritual Triad and the soul-infused personality, and has therefore seen the soul-body, the causal body or the egoic lotus totally disappear, being no longer of any true importance. There is a peculiar and at present inexplicable relation between this system of nadis and the antahkarana when it is in process of creation or is created.

6. The physical body, therefore, like so much else in nature, is itself triple in design. There is:

    a. The etheric body.

    b. The substantial nadis.

    c. The dense physical body.

These form one unit and in incarnation are inseparable.

7. The centres in their totality and the many focal points of contact found in the etheric body are responsible for the creation and preservation of the endocrine glandular system in a form either limited and inadequate, or representative of the spiritual man and entirely adequate. The nadis, in their turn.

are responsible for the creation and precipitation of the twofold nervous system. This is a point most carefully to be borne in mind and is the clue to the problem of creativity.

8. The type of the etheric substance "substanding" any form is dependent upon two factors:

   a. The kingdom of nature concerned. Basically the four kingdoms draw their pranic life each from one or other of the four levels of etheric substance, counting upwards from the lowest:

      1. The mineral kingdom is sustained from plane 1.
      2. The vegetable kingdom is sustained from plane 2.
      3. The animal kingdom is sustained from plane 3.
      4. The human kingdom is sustained from plane 4.

      That was the original condition; but as evolution proceeded and there was an inter-acting emanation established between all the kingdoms, this automatically changed. It was this "esoteric emanating change" which, aeons ago, produced animal-man. I give this as an illustration and a key to a great mystery.

   b. Curiously enough, in the human kingdom (and only in the human kingdom) the etheric body is now composed of all four types of etheric substance. The reason for this is that eventually (when mankind is spiritually developed) each of these four planes or types of etheric substance will be responsive to the four higher levels of the cosmic physical plane—the etheric levels, to which we give the names: the logoic level, the monadic, the atmic level and the buddhic. This will happen as a result of *conscious* growth and initiation.

9. It must also be remembered that the substance of which these etheric channels or channelling tubes are composed is planetary prana, the life-giving, health-giving energy of the planet itself. Through these tubes, however, may flow all or any of the possible energies—emotional, mental, egoic, manasic, buddhic or atmic, according to the point in evolution which the man concerned has reached. This always means that several energies are pouring through these tubes, unless the point in evolution is exceedingly low or unless one is dealing with a cleavage; these various energies are fused and blended together but find their own focal points in the etheric body when entering directly within the circumference of the dense physical body. Just as it can be said of the soul or of the Deity, so it can be said of the energetic or vital etheric body or entity: "Having pervaded this whole universe with a fragment of myself, I remain."

The word "prana" is almost as much misunderstood as are the words "etheric" or "astral." It is this loose connotation which is responsible for the great ignorance prevalent in occult circles.

Prana might be defined as the life-essence of every plane in the sevenfold area which we call the cosmic physical plane. It is the LIFE of the planetary Logos, reduced within limits, animating, vivifying and correlating all the seven planes (in reality the seven subplanes of the cosmic physical plane) and all that is to be found within and upon them. The cosmic sutratma or life-thread of the planetary Logos enters His manifestation on the highest of our planes (the logoic plane) and, through the instrumentality of the in-forming Lives to be found in Shamballa (which, I must remind you, is *not* the name of a locality) is brought into contact with, or is related to, the matter of which the manifested worlds are made—formless, as on the cosmic etheric planes (our highest four planes), or tangible and objective, as on the lower three planes. The fact that we call only that tangible which we can see or touch and contact through the medium of the five senses is entirely wrong. *All* is regarded as belonging to the world of form which is found on the physical plane, the astral plane and the levels of the lower mind. This lower mental plane, referred to above, includes the level on which the causal body is found—the plane in which "the lotus of love is floating," as the *Old Commentary* puts it. All that lies above that on mental levels, and on up to the highest of the cosmic physical planes, is formless. These distinctions must be most carefully borne in mind.

There is within the human body a wonderful symbol of distinction between the higher etheric levels and the lower so-called physical levels. The diaphragm exists, separating that part of the body which contains the heart, throat and head, plus the lungs, from all the rest of the organs of the body; these are all of them of the utmost importance from the angle of LIFE, and that which is determined in the head, impulsed from the heart, sustained by the breath and expressed through the apparatus of the throat determines what the man IS.

Below the diaphragm are found organs whose use is far more objective even if of great importance; though each of these lower organs has a life and purpose of its own, their existence and functioning is impulsed, determined and conditioned by the life and rhythm emanating from the higher part of the vehicle. This is not easy for the average man to comprehend, but any serious limitation or physical disease above the diaphragm has a compelling and serious effect on all that is found below the diaphragm. The reverse is not the case to the same extent.

This symbolises the potency and essentiality of the etheric body, both microcosmic and macrocosmic, and the macrocosmic expression of the fourfold Life conditions all living forms.

Each of the four ethers, as they are sometimes called, is intended—as far as man is concerned—to be a channel or expression of the four cosmic ethers. At present this is very far from being the case. It can only truly be so when the antahkarana is built and acts, therefore, as a direct channel for the cosmic ethers to which we have given the names of universal life, monadic intensity, divine purpose and pure reason. Ponder for a while on these types of energy and creatively imagine their effect when, in due course of time and spiritual unfoldment, they can pour unrestrictedly into and through the etheric body of a human being. At present, the etheric body is responsive to energies from:

1. The physical world. These are not principles but are the feeders and controllers of the animal appetites.
2. The astral world, determining the desires, emotions and aspirations which the man will express and go after upon the physical plane.
3. The lower mental plane, the lower mind, developing self-will, selfishness, separateness and the direction and trend of the life upon the physical plane. It is

this directive instinct which, when turned to higher matters, eventually opens the door to the higher cosmic etheric energies.

4. The soul, the principle of individualism, the reflection in the microcosm of the divine intention and—speaking symbolically—being to the entire monadic expression that which "stands at the midway point," the instrument of true sensitivity, of responsive ability, the spiritual counterpart of the solar plexus centre which is found at the midway point between that which lies above the diaphragm and that which is found below it.

When the antahkarana is constructed and the higher three are directly related to the lower three, then the soul is no longer needed. Then, reflecting this event, the four etheric levels become simply the transmitters of the energy emanating from the four cosmic etheric levels. The channel is then direct, completed and unimpeded; the etheric network of light is then of great brilliance, and all the centres in the body are awakened and functioning in unison and rhythm. Then—corresponding to the directly related Monad and Personality—the head centre, the thousand-petalled lotus, the brahmarandra, is as directly related to the centre at the base of the spine. Thus complete dualism, in place of the previous triple nature of the divine manifestation, is established:

1. Monad .... Personality.
   With the threefold soul no longer needed.
2. Head centre .... Centre at base of spine.
   With the intermediate five centres no longer required.

The *Old Commentary* says, in this connection:

"Then the three that ranked as all that was, functioning as one and controlling all the seven, no longer are. The seven who responded to the three, responding to the One, no longer hear the triple call which determined all that was. Only the two remain to show the world the beauty of the living God, the wonder of the Will-to-Good, the Love which animates the Whole. These two are One, and thus the work, completed, stands. And then the Angels sing."

There is a factor bearing upon the etheric body to which very little reference has ever been made, the reason being that it would have been utterly useless information. Let me embody it in a tabulated statement, beginning with a few points earlier imparted but which should here be repeated for clarity and placed in proper sequence:

1. The planetary Logos works through the medium of the three major centres:
    a. The Centre where the will of God is known: Shamballa.
    b. The Centre where the love of God is manifest: the Hierarchy.
    c. The Centre where the intelligence of God is producing the evolutionary process: Humanity.
2. The three major centres, both planetary and human, exist in etheric substance and they may or may not produce physical correspondences. All the Masters, for instance, do not work through a physical vehicle. They nevertheless have an etheric body composed of the substance of the cosmic etheric levels—buddhic, atmic, monadic and logoic levels—and these levels are the four cosmic ethers, the higher correspondence of our etheric planes; these higher levels are the four levels of the cosmic physical plane. Until They choose, at the sixth Initiation of Decision, one of the seven Paths of Ultimate Destiny, the Masters function in Their cosmic etheric bodies.
    These three major energy centres are closely related to each other, and through his own individual major centres (the head, the heart and the throat)

the disciple is in relation with the three planetary centres. I would have you ponder on this statement for it has practical value.

3. The Monad, as you know, is to be found on the cosmic second etheric level, called the monadic plane. When the antahkarana has been built, then cosmic etheric substance can be slowly substituted for the ordinary and familiar etheric substance which "substands" the dense physical body of a man.

4. The ray upon which the Monad is to be found—one of the three major rays and, therefore, related to one of the three major centres—conditions:

    a. The disciple's absorption into one of the three departments of hierarchical work, i.e., a first ray soul will go normally into such an Ashram as that of the Master M. in the department of the Manu; a second ray disciple will pass into a second ray Ashram such as mine (D.K.) or that of the Master K.H. and therefore into the department of the Christ; a third ray soul will be absorbed into one of the Ashrams (and there are many) functioning under the Lord of Civilisation, the Master R.

    b. All who come into incarnation upon one of the *Rays of Attribute*—the fourth, fifth, sixth and seventh rays—find their way finally on to one of the three major *Rays of Aspect*. The changes of shifts in ray focus are made when the etheric body has in it an adequate measure of the substance of the lowest of the cosmic ethers, the buddhic substance; this is basic for all, on all the rays, for at the end of the age, when cosmic etheric substance composes the etheric vehicles of the initiate, the three rays become the two rays, and later another absorption takes place into the second Ray of Love-Wisdom which is the ray of our present solar system.

You can see, therefore, what conditioning factors the various energies become when appropriated and used, and how their substance, or rather the presence of certain energies in the etheric body of the personality, are essential before certain initiations can be taken. The theme is too complex to be enlarged upon here, but I would ask you to consider with care the various statements I have made and then seek illumination within yourself.

The rays are the seven emanations from the "seven Spirits before the throne of God"; Their emanations come from the monadic level of awareness or from the second cosmic etheric plane. In a certain sense it could be said that these seven great and living Energies are in their totality the etheric vehicle of the planetary Logos. The evolutionary processes can equally well be stated to be those of eliminating the physical substance lying between the dense physical body and the astral sentient body, and substituting substance of the four highest planes, the four cosmic ethers. Physically speaking, it is this etheric substitution which enables a man successively to take the five initiations which make him a Master of the Wisdom.

The first initiation is purely the concern of the man's own soul, and the moment that that initiation has been taken, a measure of buddhic energy can enter and the process of transference of the higher ethers and their substitution for the lower can go forward. This, as you may well imagine, produces conflict; the personality etheric body rejects the incoming higher ether, and thus crises are produced in the initiate's life.

Progress and initiation have been presented to us mainly in terms of character-building and of service to humanity. This approach most surely also produces conflict and the personality fights the soul. But paralleling this well known conflict, another battle goes on between the ethers composing the disciple's etheric body and the downpouring higher ethers. Of this a man is not so conscious, but the battle is a very real one, *affecting primarily the health of the physical body,* and falls into five natural stages which we call initiations. The symbolism of the Rod of Initiation teaches us that (during the initiatory process) this Rod, directed by the Christ or by the Lord of the World, as the case may be, is used to stabilise the higher ethers within the personality by an access of applied energy which enables the initiate to retain that which is from above, in order that "as above, so below."

There are three angles from which the etheric body must be considered:

1. As the mechanism which externalises itself through the nadis, or that fine system of related lines of force which, in their turn, externalise themselves through the physical system of nerves.

2. As a transmitter of many different types of energy, coming from many different sources; these energies run through or along (both words are equally true) the lines of force which underlie the nadis. A while ago I used the word "tubes," thus inferring a network of tubes through which the transmitted energies can pour; here you have a case where words are wholly inadequate and even misleading.

3. These energies—according to their source, quality and purpose—create the seven major centres which condition the many smaller subsidiary centres

and finally externalise themselves through the seven major glands of the endocrine system.

I have said earlier that the intersecting energies in the etheric body of the planet are at this time a *network of squares*. When the creative process is complete and evolution has done its work, these squares will become a *network of triangles*. Necessarily this is a symbolic way of speaking. In the *Book of Revelations* which was dictated 1900 years ago by the disciple who is now known as the Master Hilarion, reference is made to the "city which stands four-square." The etheric vehicle of the planet was inherited from a former solar system, with the purpose or intention in view of its transformation into a network of triangles in this solar system. In the next one of the triplicity of solar systems (the third or last) in which the will of God works out, the etheric body will begin as a network of triangles, but this will be resolved into a network of interlinked circles or of linked rings, indicating the fulfillment of interlocking relationships. In this present system, the result of evolution, as far as the etheric body is concerned, will be the contact established between all three points of each triangle, making a ninefold contact and a ninefold flow of energy; this is consistent with the fact that nine is the number of initiation, and by the time the destined number of disciples have taken the nine possible initiations, this triangular formation of the planetary etheric body will be complete.

The idea can be conveyed symbolically by the diagram at the side, which pictures the triangular formation and the mode of a dual growth or progression and expansion of the network because, starting with the initial triangle, two points only are left for the processes of extension.

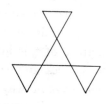

The initial triangle was formed by Sanat Kumara, and we call the three energies which circulate through its medium the three major Rays of Aspect. The four Rays of Attribute formed their own triangles and yet, in a paradoxical manner, they are responsible for the "squares" through which their energies at this time pass. Thus the work of transforming the inherited etheric body was begun and has proceeded ever since. In the etheric body of the human being you have a repetition of the same process in the triangle of energies created by the relationship between the Monad, the Soul, and the Personality.

It is well nigh impossible for man to draw or make a picture of the network of triangles and, at the same time, see them taking the circular form in their totality of the etheric body of the planetary sphere. The reason is that the whole etheric body is in constant motion and ceaseless transformation, and the energies of which it is composed are in a state of constant change and circulation.

It is wise to have in mind that it is the mechanism which changes and that this transformation of the square into the triangle has no reference whatsoever to the transmitted energies or to the various centres, except in so far that it becomes far easier for the energies to flow through the triangular formation of the etheric body than it is to flow— as is now the case—through or around a square and a network of squares.

I am quite aware that what I am here communicating may seem to you the veriest nonsense and there is, of course, no possible way in which I can prove to you the factual nature of this inter-communicating system or in which you can check and confirm what I say; but then, my brothers, you have no way as yet of ascertaining the factual existence of Sanat Kumara and yet from the very night of time His existence has been proclaimed by the Hierarchy and accepted by millions. Every human being believes a great deal more than he can prove or the validity of which he can establish.

The centres are in reality those "crossing points" of energies where the etheric body possesses seven triangles or transformed points. From the angle of Shamballa the centres in a human being resemble a triangle with a point at the centre.

From the angle of the Hierarchy, conditions are somewhat different. You have the seven centres portrayed as lotuses, with varying numbers of petals; nevertheless there is always preserved and recognisably present a triangle, at the very heart of the lotus; always there is the triangle with its communicating point, and to this we give the name, the "jewel in the lotus." You have therefore the following symbolic presentation of the lotus, and you would do well to study it with care.

The personality of the man is conditioned by the circle, which is the emanating influence of the lotus, and an interplay is thereby set up. The lotus itself is conditioned by the soul and in its turn conditions the "sphere of influence in the aura of the lotus" thus reaching into and conditioning  the personality life. The triangle is conditioned by the Spiritual Triad, when the antahkarana is built or in process of building, and in its turn first of all inspires or fires the soul, and then finally destroys it. The dot at the centre is indicative of monadic life, first of all in its lowest expression of physical life and vitality, and finally as the "point of sensitivity." Therefore we have:

1. The Point at the centre, indicative of the monadic life.

2. The related energies of the egoic lotus, conditioned by the soul.
3. The sphere of radiation, the emanating influence of the lotus, conditioning the personality.
4. The triangle of energy, conditioned by the Spiritual Triad.

The foregoing instruction on the etheric body is not long but it contains much that is relatively new and provides much food for assimilation.

IV. THE CENTRES AND THE PERSONALITY

We will now consider the centres as controlling factors in the life of the personality in the three worlds, and their relation to each other, always studying the subject from the angle of their relation to one of the three major planetary centres—Shamballa, the Hierarchy and Humanity—in connection with:

1. The Point at the Centre.
2. Related Energies.
3. Sphere of Radiation.
4. The Triangle of Energy.

The abstruseness of this theme is very great; a basic statement will, however, serve somewhat to clarify the subject; it is a statement which has seldom found expression elsewhere. Let me phrase it as simply as possible:

The centres below the diaphragm, i.e., the solar plexus centre, the sacral centre and the centre at the base of the spine, are controlled by the four ethers of the planetary physical plane; the centres above the diaphragm, i.e., the heart centre, the throat centre, the ajna centre and the head centre, are controlled by the four cosmic ethers, to which we give the names of the energies of the buddhic plane, the energies of the atmic plane, the energies of the monadic plane and the energies of the logoic plane.

This statement involves a somewhat new concept; it creates a basic relation, making possible the fact that "as above so below." Think this out. It has serious implications.

The centres below the diaphragm are—during the evolutionary process—controlled by the first, the second and the third ethers, counting from below upward; when evolution has brought the aspirant to the point of personal integration, then the energies of the highest, the etheric-atomic plane can and do control. When that takes place, then the possibility is present of the energies of the cosmic etheric planes bringing the centres above the diaphragm into full expression. This takes place upon the Path of Discipleship and the Path of Initiation. This interesting process of transference of energies is called by several names, such as "radiatory substitution," "energising at-one-ment," and "inspirational reflected light of energy." All these terms are efforts to express in somewhat inadequate words what happens when the higher energies are substituted for the lower, when the magnetic "pull" of the spiritual energies draws upward and absorbs the lower energies which are concerned primarily with the personality life, or when the reflecting light of the Spiritual Triad and of the Monadic Glory are transferred into the higher energy centres in the final vehicle used by the developed human being.

Little has as yet been given out anent the relation of the four physical ethers and the four cosmic ethers; there is nevertheless a direct relation between them, and this the initiatory process reveals. This also brings about significant changes in the vehicles of humanity. There is also a direct relation between the four aspects of karma (the Law of Cause and Effect) and the four physical ethers, as well as the four cosmic ethers; this relationship will later constitute the basis of a new occult science. Therefore, there is yet much to be grasped by students concerning energy, its emanating sources, its mode of transfer or its transitional processes, and its anchorage within the planetary body, or the physical body of the individual. With some of these

ideas we will now deal, thus laying the foundation for future
investigation, but saying little which will be of immediate
use to the individual student.

It is relatively easy to list the four cosmic ethers and
then list the four ethers of the physical plane as we know
them, and then make the statement that the average person
is controlled by the centres below the diaphragm, which are
responsive to the physical plane ethers as they transmit energies from the three worlds of human evolution, and that
the initiate is responsive to the cosmic ethers, as they play
through and awaken the centres above the diaphragm. It
must at the same time be remembered that the seven centres
in the etheric vehicle of man are always composed of the
physical ethers, but become—upon the Path of Discipleship—the vehicles of the cosmic ethers. To retain the picture with clarity, it might be well to consider very briefly
the four aspects of the centres as I have listed them above,
or that totality which they present to the eye of the See-er.
These are:

1. *The Point at the Centre.* This is the "jewel in the
lotus," to use the ancient oriental appellation; it is the point
of life by means of which the Monad anchors itself upon the
physical plane, and is the life principle therefore of all the
transient vehicles—developed, undeveloped or developing.
This point of life contains within itself all possibilities, all
potentialities, all experiences and all vibratory activities. It
embodies the will-to-be, the quality of magnetic attraction
(commonly called love), and the active intelligence which
will bring the livingness and the love into full expression.
The above statement or definition is one of major importance. This point at the centre is in reality, therefore, all
that IS and the other three aspects of life—as listed—are
merely indications of its existence. It is that which has capacity to withdraw to its Source, or to impose upon itself

layer upon layer of substance; it is the cause of the return of the so-called Eternal Pilgrim to the Father's Home after many aeons of experience, as well as that which produces experiment, leading to eventual experience and final expression. It is also that which the other three aspects shield, and which the seven principles (expressing themselves as vehicles) protect. There are seven of these "points" or "jewels," expressing the sevenfold nature of consciousness, and as they are brought one by one into living expression, the seven subrays of the dominating monadic ray are also one by one made manifest, so that each initiate-disciple is (in due time) a Son of God in full and outer glory.

The time comes when the individual etheric body is submerged or lost to sight in the light emanating from these seven points and *coloured* by the light of the "jewel in the lotus" in the head, the thousand petalled lotus. Each centre is then related by a line of living fire and each is then in full divine expression.

Much emphasis has been placed by teachers in the past upon the "killing out" of the centres below the diaphragm, or upon the transference of the energies of these centres into their higher correspondences. This I also have pointed out in other writings and instructions, because it is a definite way in which to convey essential truth. These methods of expression are, however, only symbolic phrases, and to that extent are true; nevertheless, at the close of the evolutionary process every single centre in the etheric body is a living, vibrant and beautiful expression of the basic energy which has ever sought to use it. They are, however, energies which are dedicated to divine and not to material living, and are clear, pure and radiant; their central point of light is of such a brilliance that the ordinary eye of man can scarcely register it. At this point it must be remembered that though there are seven of these points, one at the centre of each lotus,

there are only three types of such "jewels in the lotus" because the Monad expresses only the three major aspects of
divinity, or the three major rays.

2. *The Related Energies.* This expression has reference
to what have been called the "petals" of the lotus; with
these differentiations of the various energies I seek not here
to deal; too much emphasis has ever been laid upon them
both by oriental and occidental writers; there is far too
much curiosity about the number of petals in any particular
centre, about their arrangement and about their colouring
and quality. If these matters interest you, you can search in
the standard books for this information, remembering as
you garner the proffered information that you are not in a
position to prove its accuracy; its usefulness, therefore, to
you is highly problematical. I write this for real students
and for those who seek to live the life of the spirit; the information which theorists seek is amply provided for both
by me and many other exponents of the *technicalities* of the
Ageless Wisdom.

All I would remark is that as the point in the centre is
the point of life and the permanent, persistent Eternal
ONE, so the related energies or petals are indicative of the
state of consciousness which that Eternal One is able—at
any stated point in time and space—to express. This may
be the relatively undeveloped state of consciousness of the
savage, the consciousness of the average man or the highly
developed consciousness of the initiate up to the third degree, or the still more vibrant awareness of the initiate of
still higher grades. It is ever concerned with CONSCIOUS-
NESS; only the point at the centre is concerned with the
first or life aspect; the petals concern the second or the
consciousness aspect, and this must be most carefully borne
in mind.

The state of the consciousness is ever indicated by the size, the colour and the activity of the energies which compose the petals of the lotus; their unfoldment and their development is conditioned by the governing rays, as well as by the age and the length of the soul's expression. The extent and the nature of the relative "brightness" is also conditioned by the point of focus in any particular life, as well as by the trend of the thinking of the soul which is in incarnation; it must be remembered here that "energy follows thought." The natural focus or point of polarisation is at times most definitely offset by a man's line of thought (whatever that may currently be) or by the fact that he is living, consciously or unconsciously, the life of every day. An instance of this can be found in the fact that a disciple's natural focus might be the solar plexus centre, but because of his fixed and determined thought, the energy which he wields can be directed to one of the centres above the diaphragm, thus producing a temporary atrophying of the centre below the diaphragm and the consequent stimulation of that which lies above that dividing line. Thus are the needed changes made.

When the cycle of evolution is nearing its close and the initiate-disciple has well nigh run his course, the energies are all fully developed, active and vibrant, and are therefore consciously used as essential aspects of the initiate's *contact mechanism*. This is often forgotten and the emphasis of the student's thinking is laid upon the centres as expressions of his natural unfoldment, whereas that is of relatively secondary importance. The centres are, in reality, focal points through which energy can be distributed, under skilled direction, in order to make a needed impact upon those centres or individuals which the disciple seeks to aid. These impacts can be stimulated or vitalised at need, or they can be deliberately destructive, thus aiding in the liberation from substance or matter of the one to be aided.

It is high time that students paid attention to *the service angle* of the centres, and to the focussing and the use of energy in service. It is here that the knowledge of the number of the petals which form a centre is involved, because this knowledge indicates the number of the energies which are available for service, i.e., two energies, twelve energies, sixteen energies, and so forth. No attention has hitherto been paid to this important point, but it embodies the practical use of the new occultism in the coming New Age. The oriental symbols which are often superimposed upon the illustrations of the centres should now be discontinued, because they convey no real use to the occidental mind.

3. *The Sphere of Radiation.* This obviously concerns the radius of influence or the outgoing vibratory effect of the centres, as they are gradually and slowly brought into activity. These centres, or their vibrations, are in reality what creates or constitutes the so-called aura of the human being, even though that aura is frequently confused with the health aura. Instead of the word "frequently" I had almost said "usually," because that would be more definitely correct. It is the etheric body which indicates and conditions the aura, which is presumed to demonstrate what the personality is, emotionally and mentally, and (occasionally) what is indicated of soul control. This is *not* a false premise, and I would have you register this fact. It is, however, excessively limited in its import, because the aura is in reality indicative of the subject's centres. From the study of this aura certain things can be ascertained:

a. Whether the development is above or below the diaphragm.

b. Whether the centres are undeveloped or developed.

c. Whether the nature of the controlling rays is adequately clear.

d. Whether the point at the centre and the petals of the lotus are controlled, or whether a balance is being achieved.

e. Whether the personality is outgoing, and is therefore in a state of livingness, or whether a withdrawing is taking place due to introspection and self-centredness, or to the slow oncoming of the death process.

f. Whether the personality or the soul is in control, and whether, therefore, a struggle between the two is going on.

You can see, therefore, how revealing the aura can be to the individual who has the ability to read it with accuracy, and how thankful you should be that such a capacity is relatively rare, or is in the possession of an Initiate or of a Master Whose nature is LOVE.

The "sphere of radiation" is a potent instrument in service, and its extent and purity of contact should be cultivated by the pledged disciple. There is true occult teaching in the statement in *The New Testament* that "the shadow of Peter passing by *healed*." His aura was of such a nature that it had a beneficent effect wherever and whenever it touched or contacted those in his environment. The control of the Christ over His aura was such that "He knew when virtue had gone out of Him"—He knew, therefore, that healing energies had poured through one of His centres to a needy person or group of persons. It is the aura, and its potency of attraction, and its stability, which also holds a group together, which also keeps an audience listening, and which makes an individual of importance along some definite line of approach to his fellowmen. The "sphere of radiation" is easily determined by those who seek it out and who watch the effect of the radiation upon people in their community and environment. One highly emotional person, working through an overdeveloped and uncontrolled solar plexus centre, can wreck a home or an institution. I give this as an illustration. One radiant, creative life, consciously using the heart or the throat centres, can carry inspiration to hundreds. These are points well worth careful consideration. You must, however, bear in mind that these centres are brought into activity by the cultivation of certain major virtues, and *not* by meditation or concentration upon the centres. They are brought automatically into the needed radiatory condition by right living, high thinking and loving activity. These virtues may seem to you dull and uninteresting, but they are most potent and scientifically effective in bringing the centres into the desired radiatory activity. When the task is done, and when all the centres are living spheres of outgoing, radiatory activity, they swing into each others' orbit so that the initiate becomes a centre of living light and *not* a composite of seven radiant centres. Think on this.

4. *The Central Triangle of Energies*. This central triangle indicates unmistakably the three rays which condition a man's "periodical vehicles," as H.P.B. expresses it. These are: the monadic ray, the soul ray and the personality ray. To the watching and attentive Master it is also apparent which ray is the controlling ray, but this is not possible to anyone below the grade of Master. Disciples and other onlookers must form their conclusions from the "nature of the sphere of radiation." An element of error can creep in at this point, which is not possible to a Master; it must, however, be remembered that until the sixth Initiation of Decision, "the Monad guards two secrets, but loses three

when it takes control and the soul fades out." This, I may not further elucidate.

I have here given a somewhat new slant or picture of the centres. It is one of great value to students could they but realise it, because it is not truly in line with the information given to them in the occult books. An understanding of what I have said will lead the earnest student to a more practical application of his attitude to the centres, and also to a fixed endeavour to make his sphere of radiatory activity more useful to his fellowmen. The reason for this will be that his attitude will express the quality of the subjective spirit and not the quality—hitherto rampant—of objective matter. Forget not that the etheric body is a material and substantial body, and is therefore an integral part of the physical plane; forget not that it is intended, first of all, to carry the energies of the emotional and of the mental plane in the unconscious experimental stage of incarnation; that it is also intended to carry the threefold energies of the soul in the stage of *consciously* gaining experience; and that also, as the antahkarana is built, it is intended to carry the energies of the Monad in the stage of consciously expressed divinity. See you, therefore, the beauty of the spiritual process, and the planned aid given to the sons of men at all stages of their return to the centre from whence they came?

V. THE NATURE OF SPACE

Certain wide generalisations anent the etheric body should be recalled at this point. The existence of an etheric body in relation to all tangible and exoteric forms is accepted today by many scientific schools; nevertheless the original teaching has been amended in order to bring it into line with the usual theories of energy and its forms of expression. Recognition is given today, by thinkers, to the factual nature of energy (and I am using that word "factual" most advisedly); energy is now regarded as all that IS; manifestation is the manifestation of a sea of energies, some of which are built into forms, others constitute the medium in which those forms live and move and have their being, and still others are in process of animating both the forms and their environing substantial media. It must also be remembered that forms exist within forms; this is the basis of the symbolism which is to be found in the intricate carved ivory balls of the Chinese craftsmen where ball within ball is to be discovered, all elaborately carved and all free and yet confined. You—as you sit in your room—are a form within a form; that room is itself a form within a house, and that house (another form) is probably one of many similar houses, placed the one on top of another or else side by side, and together composing a still larger form. Yet all these diverse forms are composed of tangible substance which—when coordinated and brought together by some recognised design or idea in the mind of some thinker—creates a material form. This tangible substance is composed of living energies, vibrating in relation to each other, yet owning their own quality and their own qualified life. I dealt with much of this in *A Treatise on Cosmic Fire* and you would find it profitable to reread what I there said. I will not repeat it here as I am seeking a different approach.

It might be profitable to point out that the entire universe is etheric and vital in nature and of an extension beyond the grasp of the greatest mind of the age, mounting into more than astronomical figures—if that statement even conveys sense to your minds. This extent cannot be computed, even in terms of light years; this cosmic etheric area is the field of untold energies and the basis of all astrological computations; it is the playground of all historical cycles—cosmic, systemic and planetary—and is related to the constellations, to the worlds of suns, to the most distant stars and to the numerous recognised universes, as well as to our own solar system, to the many planets, and to that planet upon which and in which we move and live and have our being, as well as to the smallest form of life known to science and perhaps covered by the meaningless term "an atom." All are found existing in Space—Space is etheric in nature and—so we are told in the occult science—Space is an Entity. The glory of man lies in the fact that he is aware of space and can imagine this space as the field of divine living activity, full of active intelligent forms, each placed in the etheric body of this unknown Entity, each related to each other through the potency which not only holds them in being but which preserves their position in relation to each other; yet each of these differentiated forms possesses its own differentiated life, its own unique quality or integral colouring, and its own specific and peculiar form of consciousness.

This etheric body—vast and unknown as it is, as to its extent—is nevertheless limited in nature and static (relatively speaking) in capacity; it preserves a set form, a form of which we know absolutely nothing, but which is the etheric form of the Unknown Entity. To this form the esoteric science gives the name of SPACE; it is the fixed area in which every form, from a universe to an atom, finds its location.

We speak at times of an expanding universe; what we really mean is an expanding consciousness, for this etheric body of the Entity, Space, is the recipient of many types of informing and penetrating energies, and it is also the field for the intelligent activity of the indwelling Lives of the Universe, of the many constellations, of the distant stars, of our solar system, of the planets within the system, and of all that constitutes the sumtotal of these separated living forms. The factor which relates them is consciousness and nothing else, and the field of conscious awareness is created through the interplay of all living intelligent forms within the area of the etheric body of that great Life which we call SPACE.

Every form within the etheric body is like a centre in a planet or in the human body, and the resemblance—based upon what I gave you herein in relation to the human centres—is correct and recognisable.

Each form (because it constitutes an aggregated area of substantial lives or atoms) is a centre within the etheric body of the form of which it is a constituent part. It has, as the basis of its existence, a living dynamic point which integrates the form and preserves it in essential being. This form or centre—large or small, a man or an atom of substance—is related to all other forms and expressing energies in the environing space, and is automatically receptive to some, and repudiates others through the process of non-recognition; it relays or transmits other energies, radiating from other forms, and it thus becomes in its turn an impressing agent. You see, therefore, where differentiated truths approach each other and blend, forcing us to use the same terminologies in order to express the same factual truths or ideas.

Again, each point of life within a centre has its own sphere of radiation or its own extending field of influence; this field is necessarily dependent upon the type and the nature of the indwelling Consciousness. It is this magnetic interplay between the many vast centres of energy in space which is the basis of all astronomical relationships—between universes, solar systems and planets. Bear in mind, however, that it is the CONSCIOUSNESS aspect which renders the form magnetic, receptive, repudiating and transmitting; this consciousness differs according to the nature of the entity which informs or works through a centre, great or small. Bear in mind also that the life which pours through all centres and which animates the whole of space is *the life of an Entity;* it is, therefore, the same life in all forms, limited in time and space by the intention, the wish, the form and the quality of the indwelling consciousness; the types of consciousness are many and diverse, yet life remains ever the same and indivisible, for it is the ONE LIFE.

The sphere of radiation is conditioned always by the point of evolution of the life within the form; the correlating, integrating factor, relating centre to centre, is life itself; life establishes contact; livingness is the basis of every relation, even if this is not immediately apparent to you; consciousness qualifies the contact and colours the radiation. Thus again we are returned to the same fundamental triplicity to which I gave the names of Life, Quality, Appearance in an earlier book.* A form is therefore a centre of life within some aspect of the etheric body of the Entity, Space, where a living animated existence, such as that of a planet, is concerned. The same is true also of all lesser forms, such as those found upon and within a plane.

* *A Treatise on the Seven Rays,* Volume I.

This centre has within it a point of life and is related to all surrounding energies; it has its own sphere of radiation or of influence which is dependent upon the nature or strength of its consciousness and upon the dynamic conditioning factor of the ensouling entity's *thought life*. These are points worthy of your most careful consideration. Finally, every centre has its *central triangle* of energies; one of these energies expresses the ensouling life of the form; another expresses the quality of its consciousness, whilst the third—the dynamic, integrating life which holds form and consciousness together in one expressive livingness—conditions the radiation of the form, its responsiveness or non-responsiveness to the environing energies and the general nature of the informing life, plus its creative ability.

Much that I have given you here will serve to elucidate that which I have written upon esoteric astrology;* it will give you the key to that science of relationships which is essentially the key to astrology and also to the science of Laya Yoga. This latter science has (fortunately for the Aryan race) fallen into disrepute since later Atlantean days; it will, however, be restored and used upon a higher turn of the spiral, during the next five hundred years. When correctly and rightly restored, its emphasis will not be upon the nature of the centre involved, but upon the quality of the consciousness which distinguishes any particular centre and which will then necessarily condition its sphere of radiation. Under the great Law of Correspondences, all that I have here given or indicated can be applied by the student to all forms of life: to a universe, to a solar system, to a planet, to a human being, to any subhuman form and to the tiniest atom of substance (whatever you may mean by that last term!).

---

* *A Treatise on the Seven Rays,* Volume III.
  The Destiny of the Nations.

We shall now endeavour to apply whatever knowledge is available to you at this time in relation to the planetary Life, expressing itself as a centre in the solar system. We shall also study its secondary expression through the medium of three major centres: Shamballa, the Hierarchy, and Humanity.

The fundamental concept of hylozoism underlies all the esoteric teaching upon the theme of manifesting life. All forms are composed of many forms, and all forms—aggregated or single in nature—are the expression of an indwelling or ensouling life. The fusion of life with living substance produces another aspect of expression: that of consciousness. This consciousness varies according to the natural receptivity of the form, according to its point in evolution, and to its position also in the great chain of Hierarchy.

However, dwarfing every other concept, is the concept of life itself. There is—as far as we have ever been permitted to know—only one Life, expressing itself as Being, as responsive consciousness, and as material appearance. That One Life knows itself (if such a term can be used) as the will-to-be, the will-to-good, and the will-to-know. It will be obvious to you that these are only terms or methods organised to convey a better picture than heretofore.

This is also a brief preamble to another statement, which can be worded as follows: The planetary Logos, the One in Whom we live and move and have our being, is the informing, ensouling life of this planet, the Earth; it is His life which integrates the planet as a whole, and His life which pours through all forms—great or small—which, in their aggregate, constitute the planetary form. Preserve, therefore, in your conscious imagination and by means of the innate symbol-making faculty which all men possess, the concept of our planet as a great lotus composed of many interweaving energies, located within the greater form of the solar system which is, as we know, esoterically portrayed as a twelve-petalled lotus. This lotus, the Earth, is responsive to the many entering energies with which I dealt at some length in my book upon Esoteric Astrology.*

At the heart of this vast sea of energies is to be found that cosmic Consciousness to Whom we give the name of Sanat Kumara, the Lord of the World, the Ancient of Days. It is His Will-to-Be which brought His manifested form into *the tangible arena of life;* it is His Will-to-Good which activates the Law of Evolution and carries His Form, with the myriad lesser forms of which it is composed, on to the ultimate glory which He alone visions and knows. It is His consciousness and His sensitive response to all forms and to all states of being and to all possible impacts and contacts which guarantees the developing consciousness of all the many lives within or upon this Earth of ours.

This great Centre of Existence works through a triangle of energies or through lesser centres, each of which is brought into active expression by one of the three major Rays or Energies. The Centre which is created by the Ray of Will or Power is called Shamballa and its major activity is bequeathing, distributing and circulating the basic principle of life itself to every form which is held within the planetary ring-pass-not of the planetary Life or Logos. This energy is the dynamic incentive at the heart of every form and the sustained expression of the intention of Sanat Kumara—an intention working out as the planetary Purpose which is known only to Him.

---

* *A Treatise on the Seven Rays,* Volume III.

The second Centre is created by the Ray of Love-Wisdom; this is the basic energy which brought into being the entire manifested universe, for it is the energy of the Builder Aspect. To it we give—as far as humanity is concerned—the name of Hierarchy, for it is the controlling factor of the great chain of Hierarchy. The prime activity of this Centre is related to the unfolding consciousness of the planet, and therefore of all forms of life within or upon the planet; it is not related to the life aspect in any sense.

The task of the "units of Energy" who constitute the personnel of this Centre is to awaken and arouse the sense of awareness and of consciousness which is sensitive in its response to the life within all forms. Just as the basic mode of activity in and through Shamballa could be called the Science of Life or of dynamic livingness, so the basic science by means of which the Hierarchy works could be called the Science of Relationships. Consciousness is not only the sense of identity or of self-awareness, but it concerns also the sense of relation of that recognised self or the "I" to all other selves. This consciousness is progressively developed, and the Members of this second Centre, the Hierarchy, have the major and important task, in this particular solar systemic cycle, of bringing all the units in each kingdom of nature to an understanding of place, position, responsibility and relationships. This probably sounds entirely meaningless in relation to those conditions where the units of life are, for instance, in the vegetable or the animal kingdom, but a glimmering of understanding may come when you remember that the seed or germ of all states of consciousness is latent in every form, and of this the instinct to perpetuate and the instinct to mate are the major incubating areas.

The third Centre is that of the Human Kingdom, which is brought into being by means of the energy of the third

Ray of Active Intelligence. Its major function is intelligent creation; but it has nevertheless a secondary activity which is to relate the second and the third Centres to each other and to assume progressive control of the subhuman kingdoms and relate them to each other. This secondary function is only now assuming proportions which can be recognised and noted.

Each of these three Centres has a governing and controlling Triangle or central Triangle of Energies. In relation to Shamballa, this Triangle is composed of the three Buddhas of Activity Who represent conscious intelligent *life,* conscious, intelligent and active *wisdom,* and conscious, intelligent and active *creation.*

In connection with the Hierarchy, the central Triangle is composed of the Manu, representing loving intelligent *life,* the Christ, representing loving intelligent *consciousness,* and the Mahachohan, representing loving intelligent *activity,* and therefore between Them representing every phase of group livingness, group expression and group action; these qualities focus through the Mahachohan, primarily because He is the Lord of Civilisation and the civilisations of humanity represent progressive growth and unfoldment.

Only in the final root-race of men upon our planet will the essential central Triangle make its appearance and function openly in the third planetary Centre, that of Humanity. Men are not yet ready for this, but the areas of conscious creative activity, out of which this triangle of functioning embodied energies will emerge, is already in preparation. One point of this future triangle will emerge out of the field of world governments, of politics and of statesmanship; another will appear out of the world religions, and a third out of the general field of world economics and finance. To-day no such men of spiritual will, of spiritual love and of spiritual intelligence are to be found upon Earth; even if they did emerge in these three fields of expression they could do little good, for the sense of recognition and of responsibility is as yet inadequately developed; later, they will appear and will then openly relate the department of the Manu to that of world government, the department of the Christ to that of the world religions, and the department of the Lord of Civilisation to that of the social and financial order. That time will surely come, but it will come only *after* the externalisation of the Hierarchy and its open functioning upon the physical plane. Then, some senior disciples from each of the three hierarchical departments will appear and will attempt the experiment of this centralising and embodiment of the three qualities of the central Triangle. They will then discover, by direct action, when and if mankind is ready for such an experiment of direct control and if it has developed the needed sense of responsibility—a responsibility which will produce cooperation.

All these three Centres can therefore be depicted in the following manner: with the completed circle of the entire energy form, with the central triangle of energies carrying the qualities of the three major rays, and then the point

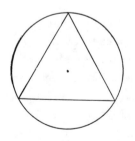

at the centre which stands for the dynamic embodied Life. In connection with Shamballa, that point is Sanat Kumara Himself; when the right time comes (though the hour is not yet) He will place His Representatives as the central points in both the Hierarchy and in Humanity. For this relatively distant event the doctrine or the theory of Avatars, of Mediators or of Inter-Mediaries is preparing the way, thus enabling men to think in these representative and inclusive terms. Not even in the Hierarchy is the time yet

ripe for the "residence in state of the divine Representative." Each year, the Buddha comes and carries the force
of Sanat Kumara to the Hierarchy, *but*—He cannot stay.
The "units of energy," the Members of the Hierarchy,
cannot bear for long the strong quality of the incoming
vibration, except after due preparation and in group form,
and then only for a few scant minutes; nevertheless the
"period of dynamic potency" is being prolonged during
this century from one day to five; the next century may see
an even longer period of registration instituted.

At the close of the age, the three major Centres will be
in complete, unified and synchronised activity, with Sanat
Kumara in Shamballa overshadowing and informing His
Representatives in the hierarchical and human Centres;
then the central Triangle in each Centre will not be only
actively functioning, but they will be working *together* in
the closest rapport, thus forming symbolically a "Star with
nine points, ever revolving"; then the massed energies of
the three major Centres will dominate the other four
centres, controlling the manifestation of the Life Expression in all the kingdoms of nature.

When one comes to the consideration of the sphere of
radiation of these three major Centres, it is interesting to
note that, at this time and in this present world cycle, the
most potent radiation and the widest range of influence
is that of the Hierarchy. Apart from "giving life" to all
forms upon and within the planet, the influence or radiation of Shamballa is definitely and consciously restricted,
until such time as the Hierarchy and Humanity can respond
constructively. It is present, needless to say, and evokes
response from those able to swing within its sphere of
radiation; but it is felt that as yet there are too many forms
of expression which could not react correctly to the work
of the "Destroyer of forms," which is the most potent

aspect of this first ray centre and the one which manifests
first, because its work must be accomplished before the
two other aspects of its potency can function rightly. The
centre called humanity has as yet an inadequate radiation
because of its—at present—inadequate development; its
sphere of influence is relatively limited, though men are beginning to work outward in the direction of the subhuman
kingdoms and to attract more forcefully the kingdom of
souls than heretofore. The Hierarchy has, however, no
interior restrictions such as are consciously and deliberately
imposed upon itself by Shamballa or which are unconsciously
imposed by humanity; any blocking of the hierarchical radiation (if I may use such a term) will come from the forms
on which the impact of its radiation is sought, but the outgoing influence of the central Triangle of the Hierarchy
is unique and far-reaching.

All that we have here been considering takes place
within the etheric body of the planet, for all these centres
exist etherically, and only etherically, and are not affected
by the fact that the "units of energy" in Shamballa or in
the Hierarchy may be functioning in physical vehicles. Some
are and some are not. The conditioning Lives in both these
Centres work entirely through etheric means, wielding and
controlling energies; the Human Centre, with its "units of
energy," works largely at present upon purely physical levels
or in the medium of that type of substance which we call
"material"; men work with outer forms, with the tangible
elements and with material factors. The "units" in the
other Centres work with substance and not with matter.
This is an interesting and vital distinction. The Hierarchy
is existent upon the buddhic plane, which is the first of the
cosmic ethers, and it works from there, impressing mental
matter. Shamballa works on the levels of the three highest
ethers whilst Humanity works primarily in the three worlds

of the dense cosmic physical plane. The New Group of World Servers has in it "units of energy" who can work both with matter and with substance.

There is here a most interesting distinction and one that is seldom grasped. Esoterically speaking, the word "matter" or material is given to all forms in the three worlds; and though the average human being finds it difficult to understand that the medium in which the mental processes take place and that of which all thoughtforms are made is *matter* from the spiritual angle, yet so it is; *substance*—technically speaking and esoterically understood—is in reality cosmic etheric matter, or that of which the four higher planes of our seven planes are composed. From the human angle, ability to work with and in the cosmic etheric substance demonstrates first of all when the abstract mind awakens and begins to impress the concrete mind; an intuition is an idea clothed in etheric substance, and the moment a man becomes responsive to those ideas, he can begin to master the techniques of etheric control. All this is, in reality, an aspect of the great creative process: ideas, emanating from the buddhic levels of being (the first or lowest cosmic ether) must be clothed in matter of the abstract levels of the mental plane; then they must be clothed in matter of the concrete mental plane; later, with desire matter, and finally (if they live so long) they assume physical form. An idea which comes from the intuitive levels of the divine consciousness is a true idea. It is noted or apprehended by the man who has, within his equipment, substance of the same quality—for it is the magnetic relation between the man and the idea which has made its apprehension possible. In the great creative process he must give form to the idea, if he possibly can, and thus the creative artist or the creative humanitarian comes into being and the divine creative intention is thereby aided.

Ideas can, however, be stillborn and abortive, and thus fail to arrive at manifestation.

The student is well aware that the three major Centres have their correspondences in the human etheric body and that each of them is related to its higher correspondence and can thus be "impressed" or affected and awakened by the corresponding higher agent. It might be stated that:

1. Energy from the planetary centre, Shamballa, utilises the head centre, the thousand petalled lotus, when the man is adequately developed. This centre is the agent of the divine will within the life of the spiritual man, working through the Spiritual Triad. It is only actively useful when the antahkarana is constructed or in process of construction.

2. Energy from the planetary centre, the Hierarchy, utilises the heart centre. This centre is the agent of divine love (expressing basically the will-to-good) working through the soul of the individual aspirant or disciple; this becomes possible when contact with the soul has been attained in some measure and the aspirant is on the way to become a soul-infused personality.

3. Energy from the third planetary centre, Humanity, utilises the throat centre, working through the *integrated* personality, and therefore only when a relatively high degree of evolutionary unfoldment has been attained. The throat centre only becomes creatively and spiritually active when the lower nature has been to some degree subordinated to idealistic aspiration; this aspiration need not be one that is usually regarded as spiritual and religious by the orthodox and therefore imprisoned thinker. It must, however, be one of which the whole integrated man

is the instrument and which will be of such a large nature that it will call all his creative faculty into expression.

In this solar system, the heart centre is the first usually to be awakened and active; as soon as there is life in that centre and a measure of activity, the other two major centres can begin to awaken. The correspondence to this can be seen in the fact that the Hierarchy is the mediating or middle factor between the planetary head and throat centres, between Shamballa and Humanity. That is why the emphasis is laid upon the heart aspect in all the teachings.

There are two centres which are regarded as "receptive and distributing agents" in an unique manner:

1. The Ajna Centre (the centre between the eyebrows) works in connection with the three major centres but mainly, at this stage of human development, as the distributor of soul force and of spiritual energy as received from the heart and throat centres.
2. The Solar Plexus Centre works in connection with the sacral centre and with the centre at the base of the spine, the centre of life; it works also with all subsidiary centres below the diaphragm, gathering and transmuting their energies and transmitting "that which has been purified" into the higher major centre.

It might here be added that the will-to-be is, from one angle, the energy of immortality; it is the energy which pours into and works through the head centre, whilst the will-to-live demonstrates as the fundamental instinct of self-preservation and is to be found positively focussed in the centre at the base of the spine. The latter is related to the personality and is closely allied to desire, and therefore to the solar plexus centre; there is a direct line of hitherto unrecognised energy between the lowest centre in the spine and the solar plexus; the other is related to the divine-spiritual man and is closely allied to the soul, and therefore to the heart centre.

The intricacy of all these relationships is most difficult for the neophyte to grasp, and this difficulty is further increased by the many and varying stages of development, of ray distinctions, and also by the numerous emphases or principles which are laid upon vehicles, upon differing planes and planetary levels of consciousness and of existence. With all this the student is not asked to deal. The factors of importance which he should attempt to realise and upon which he can construct the temple of his life and his current mode of living are simply the following—and they are the same for each and all, no matter what his ray or his point in evolution may be:

1. Man's etheric body is an integral part of the planetary etheric body and is responsive to the free distribution of the many circulating energies.

2. The three periodical vehicles which compose the expression of the human being and which make him what he is (the Monad, the Soul, and the Personality) are each related to the three planetary centres: Shamballa, the Hierarchy, and Humanity, and therefore to each of man's individual three major centres.

3. The three centres in the human being which are to be found above the diaphragm (the head, the heart and the throat centres) are the organs of reception for energies coming from the three planetary centres.

4. The agent for the distribution of the energies received via the head, the heart and the throat centres is the ajna centre between the eyebrows.
5. The agent for the purification, transmutation and transmission of the energies of all centres below the diaphragm is the solar plexus centre. It is this centre through which the majority of human beings are at this time working. It is the major controlling centre, both for the reception and the distribution of energies, until such time as the heart centre is awakening and beginning to control the personality.

There is necessarily much more to be said anent this subject of the major planetary and human centres, but I have here given the student enough upon which to ponder (I had almost said upon which to puzzle). The one important thing to be borne in mind is the *relationship* between the centres, i.e.:

1. Between the centres below the diaphragm and those above it.
2. Between the three major centres with each other.
3. Between the three major centres and the three planetary centres.

All of this must be thought of in terms of circulating and freely moving energies, distributing themselves throughout the etheric body of the planet (and therefore through the human etheric body) under the essential purpose of Shamballa and under the direction of the Hierarchy.

It is the theme of *relationship,* therefore, which is the basic pattern in the evolutionary process of unfoldment in this, the second solar system (of three systems) which is that of the Son, wherein the quality of the second divine aspect, Love, is being perfected. In this perfecting process man participates unconsciously at first, during the long cycle of evolutionary unfoldment under the Law of Necessity; but when he becomes the aspirant and takes the first steps upon the path towards spiritual maturity, he begins to play a crucial role which he maintains until he attains spiritual liberation and himself becomes a member of the Hierarchy, of the fifth or spiritual kingdom, through perfected service in the fourth or the human kingdom.

The relationship between the fourth and the fifth kingdoms is being continually increased, bringing new powers and more vital livingness into the human family which is registered by its most advanced members consciously. The distribution of energies from the Hierarchy constitutes a very interesting sequence, some of which can be indicated briefly. As we know, the Hierarchy is the Ashram of the Lord of Love, the Christ; we also know that this greater Ashram is constituted of the seven Ray Ashrams, each having at its centre a Chohan or a Master of the Wisdom; each of the seven Ashrams has connected with it one or more subsidiary Ashrams.

An Ashram is an emanating source of hierarchical impression upon the world. Its "impulsive energies" and its inciting forces are directed toward *the expansion of the human consciousness,* through the magnetic lives of the group members as they carry on their duties, obligations and responsibilities in the outer world; it is aided also by the steady vibratory activity of the members of the Ashram who are not in physical incarnation and by the united clear thinking and convinced awareness of the entire Ashram. Beginners, such as are most aspirants (though not all), are usually engrossed with the fact of the Ashram. Trained disciples are engrossed with the work to be done, and the

Ashram—as an Ashram—plays little part in their thinking; they are so pre-occupied with the task ahead and with the need of humanity and of those to be served that they seldom think of the Ashram or of the Master at its centre. They are an integral part of the ashramic consciousness and their *conscious* occupation is called, in the ancient writings, "the emanating of that which flows through them, the teaching of the doctrine of the heart which is the force of truth itself, the radiating of the light of life, borne upon the stream to which the non-initiate gives the name, 'the light of love'."

The members of the Ashram constitute *a united channel for the new energies* which are, at this time, entering the world; these energies pour dynamically through the Ashram out into the world of men; they stream with potency through the Master at the heart of the Ashram; they move with "luminous speed" throughout the inner circle; they are stepped down by those who constitute the outer circle, and this is right and good; they are delayed by the beginner and the new disciple from breaking forth into the world of men, and this is not so good. They are delayed because the new disciple has turned his back upon the world of men and his eyes are fastened upon the inner goal and not upon the outer service; they remain fixed upon the Master and His senior disciples and workers, and not upon the mass of human need.

It is essential that servers everywhere—the intelligent men and women of good will—get a grasp, fresh and clear, of the work to be done and that they become "relaying channels and not delaying points of selfish interest" in the divine flow. This takes vision and courage. It takes courage to adjust their lives—daily and in all relations—to the need of the hour and to the service of mankind; it takes courage to attack life problems on behalf of others and to obliterate one's own personal wishes in the emergency and need, and to do so consistently and persistently. However, there is much to encourage the server. Humanity has now reached a point in development where there is a definite grasp of the Plan of the Hierarchy—call it brotherhood, sharing, internationalism, unity or what you will. This is a growing and factual apprehension and is a general recognition by the thinkers and esotericists of the world, by the religious people of enlightenment, by broad minded statesmen, by industrialists and business men of inclusive vision and humanitarian insight, and even today by the man in the street. There is also a more definite recognition of emerging spiritual values and a greater readiness to relinquish hindrances to service. The plans of the Christ for humanity's release are more matured, for they had to wait until such time that the trend of human aspiration became more clearly emphatic; and the new era, with its latent possibilities can now be seen upon the horizon, stripped of the veils of glamour and wishful thinking which obscured it ten years ago. All of this is a challenge to the disciple. What is it that he must do?

The disciple has to take himself as he is, at any time, with any given equipment, and under any given circumstances; he then proceeds to subordinate himself, his affairs and his time to the need of the hour—particularly during the phase of group, national or world crisis. When he does this within his own consciousness and is, therefore, thinking along lines of the true values, he will discover that his own private affairs are taken care of, his capacities are increased and his limitations are forgotten. He takes his place with those who perceive the needs of the coming cycle—a cycle wherein the new ideas and ideals must be stressed and for which a fight must be made, wherein the wider plans for the good of the whole must be understood, endorsed and preached, the new and clearer vision for human living must be grasped and finally brought into being, and a cycle wherein the effort of all members of the new Group of World Servers must be given to the lifting of humanity's load.

There is a certain esoteric Mantram which embodies this attitude—the attitude of the disciple who is striving, in cooperative endeavour with others, to link hierarchical intent with human aspiration and thus bring humanity nearer to its goal. The intent of the Hierarchy is to increase men's *capacity for freedom* in order to function effectively with that "life more abundantly" which the Christ will bring and which demands that the spirit of man be free—free to approach divinity and free also to choose the Way of that approach. The Mantram bears the name, "The Affirmation of the Disciple." It involves certain inner recognitions and acceptances which are readily perceived by those whose intuition is sufficiently awake; but its meaning should not be beyond the ability of any sincere student and thinker to penetrate if it appeals to them as significant and warranting their effort.

I am a point of light within a greater Light.
I am a strand of loving energy within the stream of Love divine.
I am a point of sacrificial Fire, focussed within the fiery Will of God.
    And thus I stand.

I am a way by which men may achieve.
I am a source of strength, enabling them to stand.
I am a beam of light, shining upon their way.
    And thus I stand.

And standing thus, revolve
And tread this way the ways of men,
And know the ways of God.
    And thus I stand.

Training for new age
discipleship is provided
by the *Arcane School.*
The principles of the
Ageless Wisdom are
presented through esoteric
meditation, study and
service as a *way of life.*

*Write to the publishers
for information.*

INDEX

A

Adepts, telepathic work, 3, 4
Agents of directed impression, 118, 122
Alignment—
 between head centre and heart centre of planetary Logos, 132
 bodies of transmitter and recipient, 26
 brain and mind, 12
 brain and soul, 107
 brain, mind and soul, 7, 8, 12, 21-22
 effect on invocation of energies by Shamballa, 134
 evolutionary today, 132-133
 in telepathy, 26, 31
 involutionary and evolutionary, 133
Angels, effect on vegetable kingdom, 78-79
Animal kingdom,
 karma, 79
 relation to humanity, 79-80
Animal-man, production, 153
Animals, domesticated —
 bridging function, 68
 rapport with, 68
Antahkarana—
 anchoring centre, 50
 between Hierarchy and Shamballa, use, 70
 building, 51
 built by disciple, 70
 completion, results, 157, 160
 construction, 96, 107, 112, 130
 continuation through buddhic and atmic levels, 70
 effects upon soul, 165
 need for, 122
 prophecy regarding, 139
 relation to head centre, 190
 relation to nadis, 152
 use, 97, 104, 105, 156, 176, 190
 vehicle of dynamic Will, 122
Approach to Divinity, basis, 47
Aquarian Age—
 glory of, 33
 prophecies regarding, 33, 35
Art—
 of responsiveness, 52
 solar plexus variety, 117
Artist, creative, production, 189
"As above, so below", 167

Ashram—
 definition, 194
 "freedom of", 89
 group work, lesson, 32-33
 impression from, 86-87, 88, 89, 104, 105-106
 messages from, 88
 information, 86, 87
 members, functioning, 194, 195
 of Christ, 194
 of Master D.K., 160
 of Master K. H., 160
 of Master Morya, 160
 of Master R., 160
 work, 194-195
Ashramic consciousness, participation in, 195
Ashrams—
 effect of Science of Impression, 70
 impression of humanity, 46, 194, 195
 members, senior and junior, relation between, 70
 Ray, constitution, 194
 training, 58, 59, 72-73
Aspect—
 Builder, energy, 184
 consciousness, in petals, 171-172
 consciousness, work, 180
 first or life, 171
 heart, in teaching, 191
Aspects, three divine, development and unfoldment, 125
Aspiration—
 human, linking with hierarchical intent, 197
 idealistic, subordination to, 190-191
 nature, 111
Astral—
 body. See Body, astral.
 misleading use of word, 141
 nature, freedom from, 96 ·
 plane, distortions, 102
 plane, work on by disciples, 117
 sensitive awareness, basis, 111
 world, delusions, contact with, 54
 world, energies from, response to, 156
Astral-buddhic—
 consciousness contacts in mental substance, 111-112
 nature, 111
 process, 109, 111

G

Geometrical pattern, 54, 90
Glamour—
  factor in telepathic impression, 89
  interference in interpretation, 106
  of devotees, 102
  of vertical impression, 102-103
Glands. *See* Endocrine glands.
God—
  active intelligence, impression of
    New Group of World Servers,
    46
  definition, 2
  form, substantial, 2
  intelligence, telepathic impression
    by, 46
  love, impression of Nirmanakayas,
    45-46
  mind, 43, 44, 62
  substantial form, 2
  Thinker, 119
  Will, impression on Buddhas of
    Activity, 45
Goodwill—
  men and women of, work, 195-
    196
  origin, 46
  source, 46, 47
Gospel story, keynote, 127-128
Great Illusion, definition, 138
Great Invocation, experiment, 85
Group—
  ability to work as unit, develop-
    ment, 38
  activity, good and bad, 23-24
  coherence, agency, 174
  consciousness—
    awakening, indication, 68
    in Hierarchy, 184
  Formulators of the Plan, 71
  impression, sensitivity to, 96
  individual within, sensitivity, 84-
    85
  initiation, processes, institution, 85
  invocation of Hierarchy, 82
  life of soul, 21
  love, cultivation, 37-38
  members—
    functioning in mind-conscious-
      ness, result, 6
    telepathic inter-relation, 25
  mind, training, 85
  minds and brains telepathically
    related, 7
  of disciples—
    activities, 34-35
    functioning as one, 23
    working in Ashram, telepathic
      knowledge necessary, 32-33

  of Master—
    admission to, 22-23
    and group of disciples, tele-
      pathic work between, 24
    telepathic work with individual,
      23
  purpose, training, 85
  qualities of Hierarchial Triangle,
    185
  rapport, cultivation, 37-38
  rapport of individual with, 6
  responsiveness to, learning, 8
  sensitivity, cultivation, 38
  spirit, source, 23
  telepathy. *See* Telepathy, group.
  will, training, 85
  work—
    retarding by members, 38-39
    selflessness, 39
  working in Ashram, lessons, 32-33
Groups—
  ashramic, coherence, means, 32
  impression by Hierarchy, 82
  invocative, training, 85
  new, composition and common
    meeting-ground, 1-2
  of disciples, training to invoke
    Hierarchy, 82
  reception of telepathic communi-
    cations, 42-51
  response to mass ideologies, 84
  subjective and objective, tele-
    pathic work between, 23-24
Guidance, divine, knowledge of, 121

H

Healing with auras, 174
Health, factor of substitution of
  ethers, 162
Health-giving energy of Earth, 154
Heart—
  "broken", cause, 20-21
  doctrine, teaching, 195
  to-heart telepathic work, 20
Hierarchical—
  insight, development, 56
  work, substance, 118, 119
  work, true, attitude required, 38
Hierarchy—
  and groups of disciples, tele-
    pathic work between, 24
  central triangle, 185, 188
  centre, planetary, 125-126, 128-
    129, 133-136, 137, 159, 192
  chain, 3, 122, 129, 182, 184
  cooperation with, 120
  development, 133
  direction of energies, 193
  distribution of energies, 194

NOTES